FRENCH

REAL
FRENCH
A thematic guide to fluency in speech and writing

TIM GREEN

London Paris

First published in Great Britain 1991
by HARRAP BOOKS Ltd
Chelsea House, 26 Market Square,
Bromley, Kent BR1 1NA

© Tim Green 1991

ISBN 0 245-60303-4
in USA 0-13-371766-6

Designed by Roger King Graphic Studios.
Printed in Great Britain by
Mackays of Chatham Ltd, Kent

Contents

Introduction

■ Real French

The word *Real* is fundamental to all this book sets out to achieve. To speak *Real French* must be the ultimate aim of any student of French.

There are thousands of native English-speakers who, wishing to learn to speak French, enrol on various courses, attend the relevant classes and collect all the necessary paraphernalia of books and cassettes. However, even with the best intentions, they often barely succeed in making themselves understood when the real aim all along has been a two-way conversation – communicating as they would in their native language. In order to achieve good pronunciation, a comprehensive vocabulary and contemporary phraseology, a thorough, methodical approach is required. Exposure to the language is essential, while participation and efficient learning are likewise fundamental.

This book sets out to highlight key areas of importance and difficulty – hence accelerating the learning process. However, it is a reference book, not a course book, and can only help those wishing to learn.

■ Exposure

It can be almost impossible to learn French 'in a vacuum': what the student should seek to do is to maximize his/her exposure to the language. Even visiting French-speaking countries is not necessarily sufficient, and certainly not always feasible. Listening to French radio on Sunday morning or when driving will help, while exposure to French periodicals and contemporary literature is ideal. For those fortunate enough to have access to French television, regular viewing is a must.

Exposure is crucial because it is the source of all that is naturally French – of the core idiom. Such 'real' French is not tainted by the inevitable anglicisms which result when 'converting' English into French. By using whole phrases heard on the radio, you will know what you are saying is correct. This usage is not the end result of some guessing game based on fallible grammatical rules; it is the same principle used when learning your own first language – that of listening and repeating. This emphasis on exposure will lead to the assimilation of up-to-the-minute, quality French. Such a focus on the core idiom also helps avoid anglicisms where no equivalent exists, where there is no idea-to-idea correlation at all – *bon appetit* being an obvious example.

■ Participation

It is one thing to listen to others but another to speak oneself. Being surrounded by non-French speakers in a classroom situation is not the ideal way to begin, especially when the opportunity to speak may arise for only a couple of minutes in an hour-long class. This is clearly inadequate, yet the possibility of private conversation classes may be unlikely, particularly on a regular basis. One alternative is to take up activities which involve social interaction with native speakers (contact the French Embassy or local authorities for details of French Cultural Centres). It is also a good idea to practise reading aloud while taping oneself in order to increase confidence. The aim is to speak French for sustained periods: visiting France and socializing with French people in their own environment remains the ideal.

Accent is undoubtedly the most underestimated aspect of learning French. A good French accent will induce praise within a matter of *seconds*, regardless of how good your grammar and vocabulary turn out to be! A good accent is far from easy (which is perhaps why it has been ignored by many non-native French teachers – at least until recent times). To achieve a good French accent, you must have a sharp ear and be a good mimic. However, our voices have become anglicized from birth and it is difficult to suppress this when we speak French. Learn to cast off any embarrassment or shyness when speaking and do not underestimate the importance of intonation and rhythm.

Do not worry about making mistakes since they are a natural part of the learning process. There is little point speaking French if it is limited to dull, simple constructions. Regular practice is essential and potential fluency should not be undermined by the fear of making a small mistake now and then. After all, each time an error is made, it is less likely to be repeated.

■ Efficiency

This is essential to the success of any learning process. Momentum must be kept up – if the learning process is too slow, essential grammar and vocabulary will be forgotten. Though the choice of material is to some extent subjective, the intention of this book is to highlight key areas of difficulty and usage. Tricky points are set out and 'cracked' for the reader at an early stage. Obscure slang 'to impress your neighbours' is out, common idioms and colloquialisms are in. The aim is to strike a compromise between a good grammar book and a good dictionary: the thematic format is designed to facilitate learning by means of grouping together difficult ideas and expressions in a palatable form.

The book is divided into two parts: Part One concentrates on spoken French and straightforward constructions; Part Two is concerned with written French and more elaborate constructions.

PART
1

Pronunciation

1. Give French vowels their full value by using more articulation than in English. Practise distinguishing between **le son** and **le sang**; **la dent** and **le don**; **le vin**, **le vent** and **ils vont**.

Distinguish between:

- the three *e*-sounds, as in **et**, **est** and **euphonie**
- the *u*- and *ou*- sounds, as in **rue** and **roue**
- the endings of the future and conditional, as in **j'irai** and **j'irais**.

2. **t** and **p** must not be aspirated; that is to say, they should be pronounced without the expellation of air, in contrast to English. To practise, place your hand in front of your mouth and say **tout** and **peut-être**, testing to see that you can feel no air.

3. Note the following examples of liaison:

> **c'est amusant** ("ces-tamusant"), **c'est obligatoire** ("ces-tobligatoire"), etc
> **grand homme** ("gran-tomme"), **grand honneur** ("gran-tonneur")
> **trop aimable** ("tro-paimable"), **trop excité** ("tro-pexcité"), etc
> **beacoup de vent** ("beau-coudvent"), **beaucoup de gens** ("beau-coudgens"),
>   etc
> **c'est ce que je pense** ("seskej-pense")
> **je ne le leur donne pas** ("jeune-le-leur-donne pas")
> **ce pauvre enfant** ("ce-pauvrenfant"), **pauvre imbécile!** ("pauvrimbécile"),
>   etc
> **notre enfant** ("notrenfant"), **votre ami** ("votrami"), etc
> **pas de sucre** ("pad-sucre"), **pas de chance** ("pad-chance"), etc
> **de nombreux enfants** ("de-nombreuz-enfants"), **de généreux amis** (de-
>   généreuz-amis"), etc
> **quand il arrive** ("quantil-arrive"), **quand on parle** ("quanton-parle"), etc
> **il peut arriver** ("peuttarriver")

4. Note these examples from among the many words beginning with an aspirate **h**, which do not liaise with a preceding consonant:

> **en I haut**
> **en I Hollande**
> **les I Halles**
> **un I hérisson**
> **un I hasard**

les | héros
un | hobby

5. Rhythm and intonation are important. Unlike English, each sense grouping rises in tone, only dropping at the end of the sentence. Rising intonation is also frequently used when asking a question, as an alternative to inversion or **n'est-ce pas**, e.g. **je vous la donne?**

Some tricky words to pronounce

☆ How sure are you of pronouncing these words correctly:

récemment	clown
respect	mayonnaise
la vis	l'Islande

The spelling of these words might mislead one over their pronunciation:

l'aéroport	(lie-air-o-por)
l'alcool	(al-colle)
la démocratie	(demo-cra-si)
évidemment	(evidamen)
fier (adjective)	(fi-erre)
immangeable	(ain-mangeable)
inhérent	(ee-nay-ren)
l'oenologie	(eu-nologie)
prudemment	(prudamen)
psychique	(pe-see-schique)
récemment	(raysamen)
second	(segonde)
solennel	(solanel)
le zoo	(zoh)

These words contain a 'ghost' letter which is seen but not heard:

acheter	(ash-te)
appeler	(app-le)
le banc	(ban)
condamner	(con-da-nay)
dangereux	(dange-reux *not* dangé-reux)
distinct	(distin *or* distincte)
le gars	(ga)
le jus	(joo)
monsieur	(me-sieur)
projeter	(proge-te)
le respect	(respay)
le tabac	(taba)

Here, by contrast, everything is pronounced:

la dot	(dotte)

c'est exact	(exacte)
l'impact	(impacte)
la vis	(visse)
le zinc	(zink)

English words can be stumbling blocks —

le basket	(baskette)
le clown	(cloon)
le cricket	(crickette)
une interview	(ain-ter-vee-oo *or* een-ter-vee-oo)
le jazz	(*hard j as in English*)
le short	(shorte)
les WC	(vay-say)

— though so can French words used in English:

la guillotine	(gee-o-teen)
la mayonnaise	(my-onaise)

There are some variables:

les boeufs	(beu *but* beuf *in singular*)
le fait	(fay *but* fett *before a vowel*)
les moeurs	(mer *or* merse)
les oeufs	(eu *but* euf *in singular*)
un os	(oss; o *in plural*)

With certain proper names one just has to be in the know:

Carrefour	(car-four)
Citroen	(citro-enne)
Courbevoie	(cour-be-voie)
Craonne	(cranne)
l'Islande	(isse-lande)
Laon	(lan)
Metz	(messe)
Moët-Hennessy	(moette-ennessy)
Oedippe	(ay-dippe)
Poulenc	(poo-lank)
le Temple sur Lot	(lotte)
Van Gogh	(van-gog)
Zeus	(zeusse)

Comments and reactions

☆ Test your conversational reflexes in French. If you wanted to give a swift reaction to something that had just been said, could you call to mind phrases to express these ideas?

That goes without saying.
It comes to the same thing.
That has nothing to do with it.

The expressions in this section are used to make a concise comment on something that has just been said. There are dozens of possibilities, from the incisive **tout à fait** to **bof!**, expressing a weary indifference which is well on the way to contempt.

■ I wholly agree

c'est exact	correct; that's right
c'est bien ça	that's right; that's it
ça va de soi	that goes without saying
ça se voit	that's obvious; you can tell
d'accord	all right!
bien sûr	of course
(bien) entendu	of course
certes	indeed
certainement	certainly
assurément	certainly, assuredly
manifestement	clearly, obviously
effectivement	indeed, quite so
absolument	exactly, absolutely
justement	precisely, exactly
tout à fait	quite
eh b(i)en oui/si	yes
en effet	indeed
je m'en suis douté/m'en doutais	I thought so; I thought as much
je m'en doute	I suspect so; I would think so
j'imagine	I imagine so

■ I agree to some extent

c'est selon (les circonstances)	that depends (on the circumstances)
ça dépend	that depends
c'est pareil	it's the same (thing)

ça revient au même	it's the same; it comes to the same thing
ça se peut (bien)	it's quite possible
espérons-le	let's hope so
oui, en quelque sorte	in a way; to some extent
enfin, peu s'en faut	well, nearly

■ I'm not so sure

ce n'est pas pareil	it's not the same thing
c'est autre chose	that's another matter
c'est encore à voir	that remains to be seen
je ne sais pas (, moi)	I don't know (about that)
crois-tu/croyez-vous?	you think so?
pas forcément	not necessarily

■ I don't agree

c'est inexact	incorrect; that's wrong
pas vrai/tu parles!	you're joking
(il n'en est) pas question	(that's) out of the question
(tout) au contraire	on the contrary
je n'y crois pas/je ne crois pas à cela	I don't believe it/that
qu'est-ce que tu racontes?	what on earth are you saying?
ça n'a aucun rapport	that has nothing to do with it
laisse tomber	forget it
mon oeil	you're joking; not likely; no way
allons, allons	come, come
allez!	come on!

■ I don't much care

je n'en sais rien	I've no idea
c'est normal	that's usual/typical; that's only to be expected
n'importe/peu importe	no matter
ça ne me regarde pas	that has nothing to do with me
ça m'est égal	it's all the same to me
ce n'est pas grave	it doesn't matter
laisse tomber	forget it
bof	who cares?; so what?

Fillers

A feature of articulate discourse in French is the large number of words and small word groups inserted to emphasise or to some degree colour an idea. Professional speakers - jounalists, politicians and pundits - use them extensively. In France 'plain speaking' is not seen as a virtue in quite the way it is in Britain and the United States.

☆ Try your hand at translating these phrases before consulting the lists, which group these fillers according to their function.

roughly	*by the way*
to a certain extent	*in short*
as far as I know	*all things considered*

■ firstly...secondly... - *putting ideas in sequence*

en premier/second lieu	firstly/secondly
d'abord...ensuite	to begin with...then
premièrement...deuxièmement	in the first/second place

■ roughly speaking - *approximation*

grosso modo	roughly, at a rough guess
au fond	basically, really
en gros	roughly
à peu près	more or less
approximativement	approximately
bon an, mal an	putting the good years and the bad together

■ on the whole - *generalising*

en grande partie	to a large extent
dans l'ensemble	on the whole
à tout prendre	
en règle générale	as a general rule
en moyenne	on average

■ without a doubt! - *emphasis*

sans (aucun/nul) doute	without (any) doubt
à coup sur	definitely

de loin	by far
une fois pour toutes	once and for all
de toute façon/manière	in any case, anyway
en tout cas	in any case
en tout état de cause	in any case, at all events

■ whilst it may be true that... - *expressing reservation*

dans une certaine mesure	to a certain extent
à priori	in principle
à la limite	just
à la rigueur	perhaps, possibly
à ce qu'il parait	from what it seems
de prime abord	at first glance, at the outset
éventuellement	possibly
en partie	partly

■ my own view is... - *putting forward an opinion*

dans ce cas-là	in that case
s'il en est ainsi	if this is the case
puisqu'il en est ainsi	this being so
à mon avis	in my opinion
il me semble que/...me semble-t-il	it seems to me
autant que je sache	as far as I know
autant que j'en puisse juger	as far as I can tell
..., n'est-ce pas?	
..., ou bien?	wouldn't you say?
..., pas vrai?	
..., quoi?	

■ what's more... - *adding a supporting idea*

d'ailleurs	
par ailleurs	besides, moreover
en outre	
d'autre part	
de plus	moreover
également	also, equally
parallèlement	at the same time
aussi	also
de même	similarly

en plus	in addition, what's more
au surplus	
et qui plus est	and what's more

■ however - *adding a contrasting idea*

par contre	on the other hand
en revanche	
d'une part ... d'autre part	on one hand ... on the other hand
d'un côté ... de l'autre côté	
quoi qu'il en soit	be that as it may
cependant ⎤	
néanmoins	however, nevertheless
toutefois	
pourtant ⎦	
inversement	conversely
au demeurant	for all that
en contrepoint	by contrast

■ oh and by the way - *adding a parenthesis*

au passage ⎤	
à propos	by the way, incidentally
entre parenthèses ⎦	

■ and so to sum up - *recapitulating*

en peu de mots	in a few words, briefly
en résumé	to sum up
en somme	all in all, in short
en un mot	in a word

■ in the final analysis - *concluding*

finalement	finally
en fin de compte	finally, really, when it comes down to it
en définitive	in the final analysis, finally
à la fin	in the end
somme toute	all in all
tout compte fait	all things considered, when all is said and done
(enfin) bref	in a word

Connectors

■ **Prepositions, conjunctions and associated phrases**

auprès de	compared with (e.g. **auprès de vous je ne sais rien**); in the opinion of, as far as X is concerned (e.g. **elle passe pour une rebelle auprès de sa famille**)
à mon avis	in my view/opinion (*but*: **de l'avis de la plupart des gens**, in the view of most people)
c'est-à-dire	that is to say (e.g. **le Siècle des lumières, c'est-à-dire le XVIIIème**)
chez	with, in, at the house of (also **chez Balzac**, in the works of Balzac; **c'est rare chez un enfant de cet âge**, that's unusual in a child of that age)
comme	as (e.g. **c'est comme j'ai dit**); like (e.g. **il s'habille comme lui**)
en comparaison de	in comparison with (e.g. **il obtient d'excellents résultats en comparaison de ses collègues**)
par comparaison à	in comparison with (e.g. **ces notes sont très mauvaises par comparaison à celles du premier trimestre**)
comparé à	in comparison with (e.g. **comparé à ceux de vos concurrents vos prix sont très élevés**)
par rapport à	in comparison with (e.g. **par rapport à l'hiver dernier il fait moins froid.**)
en ce qui concerne	as for, as regards, concerning, about (e.g. **en ce qui concerne vos travaux, je suis tout-à-fait satisfait**)
concernant	(e.g. **votre rapport concernant la protection de l'environnement est excellent**)
de ce côté-là	as far as that's concerned (e.g. **de ce côté-là il n'y a rien à craindre**)

devant	to, at (e.g. **il a exprimé ses regrets devant leur attitude**)
en	as, like (e.g. **il se conduit en homme**)
à l'égard de	to, towards, regarding (e.g. **il est plein de jalousie à l'égard de son voisin**)
à son égard	to, towards (e.g. **elle est pleine de prévenance à son égard**)
par égard pour	out of consideration for (e.g. **par égard pour ses grands-parents il accepta de venir à la cérémonie**)
sans égard pour	without regard for (e.g. **sans égard pour son infirmité il le bouscula**)
à tous égards	in all respects (e.g. **à tous égards cet homme est indispensable**)
à cet égard	in this respect (e.g. **la politique actuelle, à cet égard, n'est pas idéale**)
envers	to, towards (e.g. **tu n'es pas très gentil envers ton frère**)
à cette exception près	with this exception, apart from this (e.g. **il a refusé de nous accompagner au zoo; à cette exception près il était toujours avec nous**)
à l'exception de	except for, apart from (e.g. **il a tout vendu à l'exception de sa voiture**)
à part	except for (e.g. **mis à part les tableaux il n'y avait rien de valeur dans la maison**)
excepté	except for (e.g. **tout le monde, excepté vous, se plaint ces jours-ci**)
en dehors de	except for (e.g. **en dehors de la musique il ne s'intéresse à rien**)
hormis	except for (e.g. **toute la famille, hormis Etienne, partit pique-niquer**)
face à	to, towards (e.g. **quelle est votre attitude face à ce problème?**)
en matière + adjective	as far as...is concerned (e.g. **en matière culturelle ce gouvernement est très actif**)
en matière de + noun	(e.g. **en matière de musique je préfère le rock**)

de la part de	on behalf of, for, from (e.g. **une vive réaction de la part des Etats-Unis**)
sur un pied de...	on the basis of... (e.g. **sur un pied d'égalité**, as equals)
sur le plan + adjective	as far as...is concerned (e.g. **sur le plan physique**, physically speaking)
sur le plan de + noun	(e.g. **sur le plan de la communauté**, as far as the community is concerned)
en plus de	as well as (e.g. **l'instituteur leur avait donné en plus de cet exercice un poème à apprendre**)
au point de vue + noun	from the...point of view, as regards (e.g. **au point de vue efficacité**, as regards efficiency; **au point de vue rendement cette machine est formidable**)
en provenance de	from (e.g. **nous avons bu de thé en provenance de Ceylan**)
quant à	as for (e.g. **tout le monde était très gai, quant à Richard il boudait toujours.**)
en tant que	as (e.g. **elle travaille en tant qu'assistante**)
tel	like, such as (e.g. **il restait là, tel un petit garçon; on cherche un soldat, tel Mermet**)
à titre + adjective	by way of, etc. (e.g. **à titre privé**, in a private capacity; **à titre indicatif**, as a guide)
à titre + **de** + noun	as (e.g. **à titre d'exception**, as an exception; **à titre d'exemple**, as an example)
à travers	through (e.g. **on voyait trés bien la pièce à travers le rideau**)
au travers de	through (e.g. **la flèche est passée au travers du bouclier**)

à savoir	namely (e.g. **il parle plusieurs langues à savoir: l'anglais, l'allemand et l'italien**)
suivant	according to (e.g. **suivant vos conseils je suis partie en Italie**)
selon	(e.g. **selon le chirurgien il faut l'opérer immédiatement**)
d'après	(e.g. **d'après les experts ce tableau vaut une fortune**)
au sujet de	about (e.g. **j'aimerais vous parler au sujet de mon augmentation**)
à propos de	(e.g. **à propos de mon salaire j'aurai quelques remarques à faire**)
pour ce qui est de	(e.g. **pour ce qui est de mon salaire je suis très satisfait**)
à ce sujet	concerning (e.g. **j'aimerais vous voir à ce sujet**)
à ce propos	(e.g. **ils se disputaient toujours à ce propos**)
à cet effet	(e.g. **à cet effet prenons rendez-vous**)
sur	on, about, in (e.g. **sur Montpellier il y a vingt églises**, there are twenty churches in Montpellier; **sur *Le Monde***, in *Le Monde*; **ne me parle pas sur ce ton**, don't talk to me like that; **on le sent sur soi**, you feel it in yourself; **la clef est sur la porte**, the key is in the door)
vis-à-vis	opposite, compared with, towards, about (e.g, **en plein milieu du dîner il quitta la table; vis-à-vis des convives c'était très impoli**)
y compris	including (e.g. **dans sa colère il a tout cassé, y compris le poste de télévision**)
dont	including (e.g. **tous les biens, dont la maison de campagne, lui appartenaient**)

25

Lead-ins

These lists copmrise verbal 'opening gambits': common phrases for introducing an idea or beginning a sentence. They are particularly useful in the spoken language and it is a mark of fluency to have a range of these lead-ins at one's command.

☆ How would you translate these phrases at the beginning of a spoken sentence?:

> *It should be remembered that...*
> *I must emphasise that...*
> *It goes without saying that...*
> *Everything leads me to believe that...*

■ Neutral lead-ins

These bring a fact or idea to the listener's attention from a fairly neutral standpoint:

il se trouve (en effet) que + Indicative	it is (in fact) true to say that
je dois (vous) dire que	I must say that
disons (que)	let us say (that)
je vous rappelle que	may I remind you that
je dois (vous) rappeler que	it should be remembered that
il convient de rappeler que	it should be remembered that
il est de fait que	it is a fact that
je tiens à préciser que	I must emphasise/explain that
je vous signale que	I should like to draw your attention to the fact that
reste à savoir qu'il s'agisse de	what remains to be seen is whether it is a matter of
il s'agit de	it's a question/matter of
c'est une question de/il y va de	it's a question/matter of
peut-être que (or **peut-être** with inversion of verb and subject)	perhaps
notons/il est à noter que	note/it is noteworthy that
à noter + noun or **que**	note/note that
comment se fait-il que?	how is it that ...?
il s'avère que	it turns out that (n.b.: *to turn out to be* is just **s'avérer**)
je crois savoir que	I believe/understand that

il paraît/semble que + Subj.	it appears that
il me semble que + Indic.	it seems to me that
j'ai l'impression que	I have the feeling that
j'ai conscience que	I am aware that
il ressort de (+ noun) que ⎤	it emerges from ... that
il se dégage de (+ noun) que ⎦	
je vous propose que	may I suggest that
procédons à l'examen de	let us now examine

■ Persuasive lead-ins

These give your ideas a little more force. You are probably advancing your own opinion, rather than a recognised fact:

ce n'est pas un hasard si	it's not by accident that
mais ce qui n'est pas mal, d'ailleurs, c'est que	but what's not at all bad either is ...
ça n'a plus rien à voir avec	that's got nothing to do with
ça n'a pas tellement l'air de	it doesn't really seem like
je suis persuadé que	I am inclined to believe that
ce qui me frappe (également) c'est que	what I find (equally) striking is that
il va sans dire que	it goes without saying that
je compte bien que	I hope that
(il n'est) pas question de	there's no question of
force est (donc) de signaler/ const ater/etc que + Indicative	it must be pointed out/noted that
(il) n'empêche que	all the same, even if
il est bien évident que	it is quite obvious that
ça ne change toutefois rien au fait que	but that doesn't alter the fact that
je trouve bon/bête/etc que	I find it good/silly/etc that
fini le temps où...	the days are gone when...
il est (grand) temps que	it is (high) time that
il ne peut y avoir	there cannot be
il importe que + Subj.	it is important that
l'important, c'est que	the important thing is that
c'est (justement) pour ça que	that's (precisely) why
j'estime que	I think/believe that
ne serait-ce que	even if it's only
l'essentiel, c'est que + Subj.	the vital thing is
le bon sens veut que	it stands to reason that
c'est dommage que + Subj.	it is a pity that

inutile de dire que	needless to say
il est exact que	it is true/correct that
il en est/va de même pour	the same is true of
tout me porte à croire que	everything leads me to believe that

Time

It is easy to run into translation difficulties when trying to say *when* things happened or are going to happen, *how often* they happen, *how soon*, etc. Here is a range of expressions used to place an event in time, many of which incorporate special uses of prepositions like **à**, **par** and **sur**. The final section gives a selection of broadly idiomatic structures for talking about time, showing them in sentence examples.

☆ How would you convey these time ideas in French?

most of the time	*sooner or later*
in the early hours	*in just under an hour*
until very recently	*in the good old days*

■ When?

– now, nowadays:

maintenant	now
à l'heure actuelle	
à l'heure qu'il est	at the moment
en ce moment	
à présent	now, at present
actuellement	at present, at the present time
de nos jours	nowadays, these days
par les temps qui courent	in this day and age, nowadays
dans l'immédiat	
pour le moment	for the time being, for the moment
pour l'instant	

– or more precisely:

à l'instant	this instant (*e.g.* **fais-le à l'instant**)
à partir de maintenant	from now on
dès maintenant	from now on
à partir du moment où	from the moment (when)
le moment/jour où	the moment/day (when)
le moment/jour que	a moment/day (when)
à ce moment-là	at that time/moment (*past or future*)
à l'instant même	at that very moment
sur ces entrefaites	at that moment
à midi pile/précis	at noon precisely

au dernier moment	at the last moment

– or in more general terms:

n'importe quand	(at) any time
la plupart du temps	most of the time
tôt ou tard	sooner or later
un jour ou l'autre	sooner or later, sometime or other
dernièrement	lately
récemment	recently
ces jours-ci	these days (*e.g.* **il est de bonne humeur ces jours-ci**)
au départ	at the outset, at the beginning
quelques instants après	after a few moments
tout à l'heure	(*future*) in a few moments, later; (*past*) a moment ago
la veille au soir	the previous night
au petit matin	in the early hours
le lendemain au soir	the next evening
à la nuit tombante	at nightfall
dimanche passé/dernier	last Sunday
en début d'après-midi/d'année	at the beginning of the afternoon/year
en fin d'après-midi/d'année	at the end of the afternoon/year
au début de février	at the beginning of February
à la fin de mai ⎤	at the end of May
fin mai ⎦	
au printemps	in spring
par un jour d'hiver	on a winter's day
sur un an	over/during a year
les dix dernières années	the last ten years
à l'époque	at the/that time
jadis et naguère ⎤	
jadis	long ago
naguère ⎦	
au temps jadis	at one time, once
autrefois	in the past, in days gone by

■ How soon?

tout de suite	straightaway, at once, immediately
séance tenante	forthwith
au pied levé	at a moment's notice
maintenant	now

prochainement	soon, shortly
bientôt	soon
sous peu	shortly, before long
aussitôt que possible	
dès que possible	as soon as possible
dans le(s) plus bref(s) délai(s)	
sans délai	without delay
dans un proche délai	in a short time
dans les délais	within the allocated time
dans un délai de cinq jours	within five days
dans les prochains jours	in the next few days
dans le courant de la semaine	sometime during the week
sous trois jours	within three days
dans une huitaine	in about a week
d'une minute à l'autre	any minute (now)
dans une petite heure	in just under an hour
d'ici quelques minutes	in a few minutes from now

■ How often?

en permanence	permanently
sans trêve	ceaselessly
sans cesse	ceaselessly, continuously
à longueur de journée/semaine	all day/week long
tous les jours que (le bon) Dieu fait	day in day out
journellement	daily
quotidiennement	
jour après jour	day after day
maintes fois	many times
à de nombreuses reprises	many times, repeatedly
bien souvent	very often
quelquefois	sometimes
des fois	
parfois	from time to time
de temps en temps	
de temps à autre	

■ How quickly?

à l'heure	on time
à temps	in time
de justesse	just in time
à la fois	at the same time

31

en même temps	at the same time
simultanément	simultaneously
en un tour de main	in a flash
tout d'un coup	all of a sudden
en avance	
à l'avance	in advance
par avance	
tout de suite	straightaway, at once, immediately
d'emblée	right away
du jour au lendemain	overnight
tout-à-coup	suddenly
soudain	

■ Temporal conjunctions, prepositions and phrases

lorsque	when
quand	when, whenever
comme	as
pendant que	while
tandis que	while
alors (même) que	(just) when
pendant	during
au cours de	during, in the course of
durant	during, throughout
lors de	when, at the time of
tout en + present participle	while
tant que	so/as long as
jusqu'à ce que + subjunctive	until
en attendant que+ subjunctive	while
avant que ... (ne) + subjunctive	before
depuis que	since
au fur et à mesure que	as, as soon/fast as
après que	after
à peine (... que)	hardly, scarcely (... when) (*e.g.* **à peine était-il arrivé qu'il ...**)
dès que	as soon as
à partir du moment où	from the moment (when), as soon as
une fois (que)	once
toutes les fois que	every time
chaque fois	every time
au moment où	(just) as

■ Expressions

j'en ai pour un instant	I'll only be a moment
à quand tes vacances?	when are your holidays?
ce n'est que depuis une période relativement récente	it is only recently that
il a la trentaine	he's about thirty
il approche de trente ans	he's in his late twenties
il a un peu plus de trente ans	he's in his early thirties
il a trente ans passés	he's past thirty
il se fait tard	it's getting late
une année s'écoula/s'acheva	a year passed
j'ai mis deux heures pour y aller	it took me two hours to get there
tu as menti! - Jamais de la vie!	you lied! - Never!
il a disparu à tout jamais/pour toujours	he disappeared for ever
désormais/dorénavant il ne mentira plus	from now on/henceforth he won't lie anymore
(tout) d'abord j'aimerais vous présenter Dr Dupont	first (of all) I would like to introduce Dr Dupont
le match était perdu d'avance	the match was lost before it started
entre-temps elle lisait un magazine	meanwhile she read a magazine
il fredonnait un vieil air d'antan	he was humming a tune of yesteryear
la mode du moment est aux jupes longues	long skirts are the fashion of the moment
ce cours l'ennuyait à la longue	in the long run she found this course boring
la guerre existe depuis des temps immémoriaux	war has existed since time immemorial
jusqu'à une époque récente les femmes n'avaient pas le droit de vote	until recently women didn't have the right to vote
il est parti il y a quelques instants	he left a few moments ago
jusqu'alors il avait gardé son calme	until then he had kept calm
dès lors tout alla mal	from then on everything went wrong
il y a peu j'étais encore en vacances	a short while ago I was still on holiday
vivre au jour le jour	to live from day to day
travailler jour et nuit	work day and night
nous sommes le combien	what day is it today?
au gros de l'été	at the height of summer
au bon vieux temps	in the good old days
il y a belle lurette (que)	a long time ago

Causal conjunctions and phrases

These lists give words and phrases which can be used to ask why, to offer explanations and to link causes and effects.

☆ First test yourself with these five challenging translation phrases. Avoid using à cause de and be ready to alter the order of ideas to achieve a more elegant phrase in French. Answers can be found in the lists below.

> *Because of the cold she has stayed at home.*
> *He died as a result of his accident.*
> *These championships have been very friendly, because of their atmosphere.*
> *She coughs from having smoked too much.*
> *This stamp is rare, hence its price.*

■ Why?

pourquoi?	why
comment se fait-il que...?	why/how is it that...?
comment ça se fait?	why is that?
dans quel but?	why, for what purpose?
à quel titre?	why, on what grounds
	e.g. à quel titre voulez-vous plus d'informations?

■ Because

c'est que	it's because
du fait que	on account of, as a result of
étant donné que	given that
comme	since
puisque	since
vu que	seeing that
vu + noun	in view of
à force de	by, through
	e.g. il a gagné à force d'avoir beaucoup travaillé
parce que	because
car	for
(c'est) à cause de	because of, due to
en raison de	because of
	e.g. en raison du froid, elle est restée chez elle

par suite de	as a result of
	e.g. **il est mort par suite de son accident**
de par	because of
	e.g. **ces championnats ont été, de par leur ambiance, très sympathiques**
par le fait (même) que	(precisely) due to the fact that
de	from
	e.g. **elle tousse d'avoir trop fumé**
en	because of it
	e.g. **ils criaient si fort qu'ils en perdaient la voix,** they shouted so loud that they lost their voices
grace à	thanks to
d'autant (plus) ... que	all the more so because
	similarly: **il y a d'autant moins de policiers qu'ils ne sont pas bien payés,** there are much fewer police officers because they are not well paid

■ Therefore

donc	therefore
c'est pour ça que	
c'est pourquoi	that's why
voilà pourquoi	
ce qui fait que	which means that
ça fait que	that means that
d'où	hence
	e.g. **ce timbre est rare, d'où son prix**
aussi	therefore
	e.g. **je suis faible, aussi ai-je besoin d'aide**
raison de plus (pour faire)	all the more reason (for doing)

■ In order to

pour que	so that
afin que	
de (telle) sorte/manière/façon que	so that, in such a way that
en sorte que	

en vue de	with a view to
dans le but de	with the aim of

■ Causal verbs and verb phrases

entraîner ⎤	
occasionner	to cause, lead to
causer	
produire ⎦	
provoquer	to cause, provoke
	e.g. **la pluie a provoqué de grandes inondations**
susciter	to cause, arouse
faire naître	to cause, give rise to
aboutir à	to lead to, result in
être à l'origine de	to be the root/cause of
être lié à	to be linked to/connected with
tenir à	to be due to, stem from
survenir	to arise, occur
arriver	to happen, occur
résulter	to result in
	e.g. **il en est résulté une réduction des bénéfices**
résulter de	to result from
	e.g. **il résulte de l'inflation une baisse du niveau de vie**
s'ensuivre	to follow, to ensue

Nouns

French has limited scope for creating compound nouns. English can simply fuse two words to make a new one, e.g. *lipstick*; in French we spell it out: **rouge à lèvres**.

This is a list of everyday nouns — *dashboard, toaster,* etc. — which can only be conveyed in French by a hyphenated compound or a group of words.

april showers	**les giboulées de mars**
bagpipe	**la corne-muse**
beetroot	**la betterave rouge**
birthday party	**la fête d'anniversaire**
black eye	**un oeil au beurre noir**
bunch of grapes	**la grappe de raisin**
bunch of keys	**le trousseau de clefs**
chest infection	**la fluxion de poitrine**
close up	**le gros plan**
commuter town	**la ville-dortoir**
dashboard	**le tableau de bord**
dinner, evening meal	**le repas du soir**
doctors' surgery	**le cabinet de médeçin**
dormer window	**le chien-assis**
finger mark	**une trace de doigt**
fingerprint	**une empreinte digitale**
floor (lino)	**le sol de lino**
floor (stone)	**le sol dallé**
floor (tiled)	**le carrelage**
freckle	**la tache de rousseur**
french window	**la porte-fenêtre**
grape	**le grain de raisin**
head office	**le siège social**
kerb	**la bordure du trottoir**
launderette	**la lavarie automatique**
lipstick	**le rouge à lèvres**
lunch, midday meal	**le repas de midi**
main course	**le plat de résistance**
make-up	**le fond de teint**
market day	**le jour de foire**
packed lunch	**le panier-repas**
password	**le mot passe-partout**

pram	la voiture d'enfant
raisin	le raisin sec
(registered) trademark	la marque déposée
roadblock	le barrage de police
sand bank	le banc de sable
search warrant	le mandat de perquisition
sightseeing boat	le bateau-mouche
soft toy	le jouet en peluche
solicitors' practice	une étude de notaire
sticker	un auto-collant
teddy (bear)	un ours en peluche
toaster	le grille-pain
toothpaste	la pâte dentifrice
vegetable garden	le jardin potager
vest	le gilet de corps
walkie-talkie	le talkie-walkie
windowsill	le rebord de la fenêtre

Prepositions

Perhaps because they're small, prepositions get all over the place! And some of the uses are quite surprising: **sur** doesn't always translate as *on* and **de** doesn't always mean *of*. These lists group some of these unexpected uses.

☆ Try translating these short phrases. As you've guessed, the literal translation of the preposition is the one to avoid.

> *under no circumstances*
> *on a day like this*
> *in this photo*
> *a survivor of the war*

■ à

à pied d'oeuvre	ready to get down to the job
à des conditions difficiles	on difficult terms, in difficult conditions
à tout prix	at all costs
une femme à l'air heureux	a happy-looking woman
la maison à la cheminée blanche	the house with the white chimney
à votre guise/gré	as you please
contre votre gré	against your will
à contrecoeur	reluctantly
à l'encontre de qqch/qqn	against sth/against someone's will
au dernier étage	on the top floor
à leur insu	without their knowledge
au total	all in all, in total
à tour de rôle	in turn
un survivant à la guerre	survivor of the war
à votre place	if I were you
petit à petit	little by little
peu à peu	gradually
au passage	by the way, in passing
au loin	in the distance
amarré au large de Long Beach	anchored off Long Beach
des pieds à la tête	from head to toe
posé à même le sol	put level with the ground
au soleil	in the sun
au gros de la saison	at the height of the season

■ avec

avec désinvolture   casually; in an offhand way

■ contre

contre votre gré   against your will
fâché contre   angry with
six voix contre deux   six votes to two

■ dans

dans la feuille   on the sheet (of paper)
dans le vent   in fashion
dans le lointain   in the distance

■ de

une réputation de bonne chère a reputation for good food
de tout mon coeur   with all my heart
de mon plein gré   of my own free will
de gré ou de force   whether you like or not
le long de   along
les maisons d'en face   the houses opposite
des pieds à la tête   from head to toe

■ en

en aucune circonstance   under no circumstances
en bon état   in good condition, tidy
en première question/heure as the first question/in the first hour
en tout   in all
en manches de chemise   in shirtsleeves
les maisons d'en face   the houses opposite
en montagne   in the mountains
en tous sens   in all directions

■ entre

entre chien et loup   in the twilight

■ par

se pencher par la fenêtre   to lean out of the window
par un jour pareil   on a day like this

par plaisanterie	for a joke
par-dessus le marché	into the bargain

■ **parmi**

blotti parmi les arbres	nestling amongst the trees

■ **pour**

pour dernier cours	for the last lesson

■ **sous**

sous un soleil étouffant	in the stifling summer heat
sous la pluie	in the rain

■ **sur**

sur le vif	from life, in real life
sur ma gauche/droite	on my left/right
sur la place/le boulevard/l'avenue	in the square/boulevard/avenue (*but* **dans la rue** in the street)
sur cette photo	in this photo
sur la pointe des pieds	on tiptoe
sur la place/le parking	in the square/car park
juché sur un escabeau	perched on a stool
crispé sur le fauteuil	on the edge of your seat

Verbs

The verbs in these lists often crop up in argued speech or writing, be it journalism or essay. The categories are broadly thematic. All the verbs are abstract and they offer expressive alternatives to simpler verbs like **dire** or **penser**.

■ Expressing

aborder	to tackle, approach
affirmer	to assert
faire appel à	to appeal to, call upon
confier qch à qqn	to confide sth. to so.
se confier à	to confide in
conspuer	to boo
convoquer	to call, summon
crier	to shout
also **s'écrier**	
détailler	to spell out, detail
être en désaccord fondamental	to disagree fundamentally
en dire autant	to say the same
discuter	to discuss
s'enliser	to get bogged down
s'exclamer	to exclaim
s'excuser (de qch)	to apologise (for sth.)
s'expliquer	to explain oneslf; to talk things over
faire valoir	to put forward, assert
inciter qqn à faire qch	to encourage so. to do sth.
interpeller	to shout out; to question
se mettre d'accord	to come to an agreement
mettre (deux choses) en parallèle	to compare (two things) directly
mettre le doigt dessus	to put one's finger on it
mettre qn au courant de qch	to tell so. about sth.
mettre/remettre en cause	to call into question
parler à tort et à travers	to talk nonsense
porter sur	to concern, focus on
préciser	to specify
préconiser	to advocate
prôner	to extol, advocate
prendre parti	to take sides
se prononcer pour	to come out in favour of

quémander	to beg for
rabrouer	to rebuff
réclamer	to claim
résumer	to sum up
revendiquer	to claim
signaler/faire remarquer	to point out
soutenir	to maintain
traiter (de)	to deal with
traiter qn de...	to call someone a...

e.g. **il m'a traité de lâche,** he called me a coward

■ Feeling

s'affoler	to panic
aspirer à	to aspire to
attendre avec impatience	to long for/to
avoir très envie de	to long for/to
avoir confiance en	to trust
faire confiance à	to trust
se contenter de	to be satisfied with
se crisper	to become tense
déprimer	to get depressed
se détendre	to relax
se douter de	to suspect
douter de	to doubt
être enclin à	to be inclined to
s'ennuyer	to be bored
éprouver	to experience, feel
espérer vivement	to hope strongly
se fatiguer	to get tired
se fier à	to trust
avoir foi en	to have faith in
se griser de	to be intoxicated by, be carried away by
se méfier de	to distrust, be suspicious of
mépriser	to scorn, despise
se mettre en colère	to get angry
se passionner pour	to have a passion for
prêter une importance excessive à	to overrate
se raviser	to change one's mind
se réjouir de	to be delighted to/about
se soucier de	to be worried about

souhaiter vivement	to very much hope for
avoir soupçon que	to suspect that
avoir tendance à	to tend to
tenir à	to be attached to, be fond of
toucher	to touch, affect

■ Thinking

s'affairer à	to busy oneself
tenir compte de	to take into account
s'y connaître à/en	to know all about
constater	to observe
être au courant de qch	to know about sth.
se dévouer à	to dedicate/devote oneself to
prendre une décision	to make/take decision
	i.e. not "**faire une décision**"
estimer que	to think that, believe that
faire face à	to face (up to)
ignorer	to be unaware of, have had no experience of
	cf. possible translations of *to ignore*:
	faire semblant de ne pas apercevoir
	ne tenir aucun compte de
	ne pas prêter attention à
	ne pas relever
insister pour faire qch	to insist on doing sth
avoir les pieds sur terre	to have one's feet on the ground
faire le point	to take stock, sum up
être porté à croire que	to be led to believe that
réfléchir	to consider
se rendre compte de	to realize
retenir	to remember
scruter	to examine
travailler	to work on (an essay etc.)
viser à	to aim to

■ Doing

s'acheminer vers	to proceed towards
chambouler	to make a mess of
démissioner	to resign
se débarrasser de	to get rid of
s'éloigner de	to distance oneself from
s'entretenir	to make a living

être au bon endroit au bon moment	to be in the right place at the right time
faire de son mieux	to do one's best/utmost
faire son possible	to do one's best/utmost
faire des progrès	to make progress
faire en sorte que	to see to it that
s'immiscer dans	to interfere in
impliquer dans	to implicate (someone) in
avoir du mal à faire qch	to have difficulty doing sth
se mêler de	to meddle in
mettre en pratique/appliquer	to put into practice
mettre qch au point	to elaborate/perfect sth
passer à l'action	to take action
se perdre	to get lost
mettre qch en pratique	to put sth into practice
prendre l'habitude (de)	to get into the habit (of)
profiter de l'occasion (de faire)	to make use of the opportunity (to do)
régler	to settle sort out
rémédier à	to resolve
renvoyer	to postpone
reprendre	to resume, take up again
se ruer	to rush, fling oneself
saisir l'occasion par les cheveux	to seize the opportunity with both hands
tenir le coup	to hold out

■ Happening

aboutir à	to end at, lead to
aller bon/grand train	to make good progress
arriver	to happen
avoir lieu	to take place
décoller	to take off
être en train	to be underway
intervenir	to take place; (of decision) to be taken
prendre son envol	to take off
se dérouler	to take place, pass off
se passer	to take place, happen
se poursuivre	to continue, go on
se produire	to happen, occur
se tenir	to be held
tirer à sa fin	to draw to a close, come to an end
tomber à l'eau	to fall through
trouver une fin	to draw to a close, come to an end

Adjectives

These lists focus mainly on abstract adjectives: the type that usually come *least* easily to hand when you want them. Where feminine forms are not shown the feminine is made in the usual way, by adding -e if the word does not already end in -e.

☆ Could you describe someone in French as

brawny and weatherbeaten
starchy and forbidding or
neurotic and unpredictable

■ Describing people

I Physical appearance

aguichant	enticing, alluring
avachi	limp, sloppy, baggy
baraqué	well-built
bizarre	strange
boursouflé	bloated
bronzé	sunburnt
chétif, -ive	weak, puny
débraillé	untidy, sloppy, slipshod
dépenaillé	unkempt
douteux, -euse	doubtful, dubious, questionable
élancé	slim
frêle	frail, fragile
grand	tall
grassouillet, -ette	plump
gros, grosse	fat
hâlé	weather-beaten
insolite	unusual
maigre	skinny
mignon	nice, sweet
mince	thin
musclé	brawny, muscular
nerveux	nervous; upset
pâle	pale
potelé	plump
rabougri	wizened, shrivelled
séduisant	attractive, appealing, seductive

II Character

abruti	idiotic
acariâtre	sour, cantankerous
antipathique	unfriendly
anodin	harmless
astucieux, -euse	shrewd
atone	lifeless, expressionless
avisé	sensible, wise
borné	narrow-minded
braillard	noisy
brave	good, honest
candide	naive, ingenuous
casanier, -ière	stay-at-home
compassé	starchy, stiff
compliqué	complicated; fussy (e.g. about food)
compréhensif, -ive	understanding
dépravé	degenerate
dévoyé	delinquent
difficile	difficult, tiresome
distrait	absent-minded
drôle	funny
ennuyeux, -euse	boring
évolué	broad-minded, independent, progressive
exigeant	demanding
extraverti	extrovert
faiblard	weak, feeble, slow on the uptake
fainéant	lazy, idle
falot	dreary
farfelu	hare-brained, eccentric
franc	candid
futé	cunning, smart
guindé	stilted, stuffy
imprévisible	unforeseeable
juste	fair
lunatique	temperamental
maladroit	clumsy
mal commode	bad-tempered
malicieux, -euse	mischievous, naughty
malin	smart, clever
malveillant	malicious, malevolent, spiteful
maniaque	finicky, fussy

47

marrant	funny; odd
maussade	gloomy, sullen
méchant	malicious, nasty
méfiant	distrustful, suspicious
méprisant	contemptuous, disdainful
pas naturel, -elle	affected, mannered
névrosé	neurotic
perspicace	perceptive, shrewd
primesautier, -ière	impulsive
rébarbatif, -ive	forbiding, off-putting
renfrogné	sullen
replié sur soi-même	introverted
rusé	cunning
sage	well-behaved, good
saugrenu	preposterous
sensé	sensible
sensible	sensitive
sérieux, -euse	serious, responsible
susceptible	touchy, sensitive
sympathique	nice, friendly
terre-à-terre	down-to-earth
tordu	warped
travailleur, -euse	hard-working

III Mood

accablé	distressed
admiratif, -ive	admiring
affolé	in a panic
amer, -ère	bitter
assoupi	drowsy
béat	blissful; smug, complacent
cafardeux, -euse	in the dumps
débordé (de travail)	snowed under (with work)
décontracté, détendu	relaxed
découragé	disheartened
dépité	vexed
désemparé	distraught, at a loss
effaré (de)	alarmed (at)
énergique	energetic
enthousiaste	enthusiastic
gai	cheerful
bien intentionné	well-intentioned

lointain	distant
mélancolique	gloomy
navré	sorry, apologetic, upset
paumé	lost, at sea
ravi	delighted
surpris	surprised
tendu	tense
vanné	deat beat, exhausted
vexé	annoyed

■ Describing ideas or events

I Positive

alléchant	tempting, mouth-watering
attendrissant	touching
bénéfique	beneficial
commode	convenient
cocasse	droll, comical
conforme (à)	conforming (with)
convenable	fitting, acceptable, respectable
déroutant	disconcerting
détaillé	comprehensive
distinct	separate, distinct
équitable	fair
excellent	excellent, first-rate
formidable	fantastic, tremendous
fulgurant	dazzling
grave	serious
honnête	decent
hors pair	exceptional
impeccable	great, smashing
important	important; considerable, sizable
marrant	funny
merveilleux	marvellous
parfait	great, fine
passionant	exciting
percutant	forceful
primordial	of prime importance
propice	favourable
	(Note also: **c'est très propice à une attaque ici,** you are very liable to be attacked here)

49

raisonnable	reasonable
rarissime	extremely rare
recherché	much sought-after; studied
réconfortant	comforting
réjouissant	delightful
rentable	profitable, financially viable
réussi	successful, well-done
sagace	sagacious
sage	wise
sensationnel	sensational
spontané	spontaneous
subtil	subtle
surprenant	surprising
véridique	truthful

II Negative

aberrant	absurd, nonsensical
abominable	abominable
affreux	dreadful, ghastly
agaçant	irritating
aléatoire	uncertain, random
ardu	arduous
chimérique	fanciful, imaginary
complexe	complex
courant	common, current
déchirant	heart-breaking
dégoûtant	disgusting
déprimant	depressing
déraisonnable	unreasonable
discutable	questionable, arguable
écoeurant	sickening
ennuyeux, -euse	boring
épouvantable	frightful
éprouvant	strenuous, exacting
étrange	strange
fastidieux, -euse	tedious, dull
frustrant	frustrating
gênant	annoying
immonde	filthy
impensable	unthinkable
impossible	difficult; impossible
improbable	unlikely

inadmissible	intolerable
inattendu	unexpected
loufoque	nuts, crazy
lourd	gross, dull
malaisé	difficult
malencontreux, -euse	unfortunate, awkward, untoward
médiocre	mediocre
minable	seedy, hopeless, pathetic
minant	boring, deadly
pénible	difficult, tiresome; painful
pitoyable	pathetic
prosaïque	prosaic
quelconque	ordinary, mediocre
rebutant	off-putting
répugnant	repugnant
ridicule	ridiculous
sclérosé	ossified, hidebound

Some Idiomatic Expressions

Once you've been working with French for a year or two, you begin to encounter words used in ways that are surprisingly different from their first and commonest senses. "So *that's* how you say that in French", one thinks. "I must try to remember that."

A full list of these secondary and often idiomatic uses would be practically endless, though here are a few that should increase fluency.

s'aider	**il s'aide d'une canne pour marcher,** he uses a walking-stick
argent	**tu en as pour ton argent,** you got your money's worth
arranger	**ça n'arrange rien,** that doesn't help
automatisme	**c'est un automatisme,** I do it instinctively
bain	**j'ai pris un bain de jouvence,** it's made me feel years younger
beau fixe	**nos relations restent au beau fixe,** we're the best of friends
bien	**c'était aussi bien,** that was as well
bloquer	**je suis bloqué,** I'm stuck
borne	**tu dépasses les bornes,** you're going to far
chance	**vous ne mesurez pas la chance que vous avez,** you don't realise how lucky you are
chandelle	**je lui dois une fière chandelle,** I owe him a debt of gratitude
chercher	**il cherche midi à quatorze heures,** he's looking for complications
chic	**ce n'est pas très chic de ta part,** that's not very nice of you
clocher	**qu'est-ce qui cloche?,** what's wrong?

coeur	**ça me tient au coeur,** it means a lot to me **je la connais par coeur,** I know her inside out
coin	**tout le monde se retrouvera au bistrot du coin,** everyone is going to meet up at the local pub
comblé	**je suis comblé,** I'm very flattered
dépouillé	**il est dépouillé de tout préjugé,** he is completely without prejudice
déroulement	**voilà le déroulement,** that's what is going to happen
dire	**cela vous dit de sortir?,** do you feel like going out? **cela ne me dit rien,** I don't feel like it; I don't fancy the idea
se dire	**il se dit scientifique,** he claims to be a scientist
donner	**ce n'est pas donné,** they're hardly giving it away **qu'est-ce que cela donne, ton jardin?** how is your garden doing? **on va voir ce que cela donne,** we're going to see what happens
douter	**on ne saurait douter de ses qualités,** you couldn't deny his qualities
emballer	**ça ne m'emballait pas de l'essayer,** it didn't encourage me to try it
embarrasser	**est-ce qu'il y a des mots qui vous embarrassent?,** are there any words you're having trouble with?
encre	**cela a fait couler beaucoup d'encre,** a lot has been written about this
s'enterrer	**pendant trois jours je me suis enterré à la campagne,** for three days I buried myself in the country
esprit	**ça ne me revient pas à l'esprit,** I can't remember
facilement	**on reste facilement au lit quand il fait froid,** it is easy to stay in bed when it is cold

faire	**rien n'y fait,** it makes no difference; it's no use
foncer	**on fonce!,** let's get down to it; let's get to work
frime	**c'est pour la frime,** it's all for show
gabarit	**ce n'est pas le petit gabarit,** he's not exactly small
gâteau	**c'est du gâteau/de la tarte,** it's a piece of cake
genre	**ce n'est pas mon genre,** it's not my kind of thing
gonflé	**tu es gonflé,** you've got a nerve!
grand-chose	**il n'y a pas grand-chose à signaler,** there's not much worth pointing out **il n'a pas dit grand-chose,** he didn't say a lot (avoid **beaucoup**)
haricots	**c'est la fin des haricots,** that's the last straw; that's all we needed (*ironic*)
intérêt	**ça n'a pas beaucoup d'intérêt,** that isn't very interesting
jour	**décidément, c'est mon jour,** it's just not my day today
latin	**j'y perds mon latin,** I can't make head or tail of it
mal	**ce n'est pas si mal que ça,** it's not as bad as all that **ça ne me ferait pas de mal,** it wouldn't do me any harm
malin	**ce n'est pas plus malin que ça,** it's as simple as that
meilleure	**c'est la meilleure!** like hell!
mer	**ce n'est pas la mer à boire,** it's not impossible
moins	**je n'en pense pas moins,** I'm thinking about it even so
monde	**ce n'est pas la fin du monde,** it's not the end of the world
mûrir	**ses expériences l'ont mûri,** he has learnt from his experiences

pas de quoi	**il n'y a pas de quoi faire une histoire,** it's nothing to make a song and dance about
se passer	**que s'est-il passé?,** what's happened?
pavoiser	**pas de quoi pavoiser,** it's nothing to write home about
pieds	**ça me casse les pieds,** that really annoys me
poil	**il s'en est fallu d'un poil,** it was a close shave/thing **ça me va au poil,** that suits me fine
point	**tu n'iras pas, un point c'est tout,** you are not going and that's that
pour cent	**je ne suis pas sûr à cent pour cent,** I'm not 100% certain
prendre	**qu'est-ce qui t'a pris?,** what got into you?
quoi	**on a déjà de quoi faire,** we already have a lot to do
saint	**il ne savait pas à quel saint se vouer,** he didn't know which way to turn
schématiser	**je schématise un peu,** I'm simplifying it a bit
tête	**je ne l'ai plus en tête maintenant,** I can't remember **il ne savait où donner de la tête,** he didn't know whether he was coming or going/what to do next
trop	**on ne le sait que trop,** we know (it) only too well
valoir	**je les vaux bien,** I'm as good as they are **ça ne lui a rien valu,** it didn't do him any good
vent	**c'est du vent,** it's all hot air
vie	**qu'est-ce que vous faites dans la vie?,** what do you do for a living?
yeux	**ça ne vous coûte pas les yeux de la tête,** it won't cost you the earth

Etiquette

Bonjour and **bonsoir** are almost invariably followed by **Monsieur, Madame or Mademoiselle** if the relationship is one of some formality, i.e. someone you would not address by their Christian name. For informal greetings, **salut** is as universal as *hi* in English.

■ How are you?

comment allez-vous, comment vas-tu?	how are you?
ça va?	
ça marche?	
vous avez bien dormi?	did you sleep well?

■ Fine, so-so, not so good...

très bien, merci et vous/toi?	very well, thank you - and you?
oui, ça va	yes, I'm fine
non, pas tellement	not too good (i.e. in answer to **ça va?** etc...)
comme ci, comme ça	so-so, fair to middling
coussi, coussa	so-so (informal)
ça peut aller	could be worse
je vais bien	I'm well/healthy
je suis en pleine forme	I'm in great shape

■ Yes please, no thank you

je veux bien	yes please
volontiers	gladly, sure
c'est très gentil à vous	that's very kind of you
ça me ferait plaisir	I'd be delighted
non merci	no thank you
plus rien, merci	no more, thank you
merci (à vous)	thank you
je vous remercie (beaucoup)	thank you (very much)
merci bien/beaucoup	thank you very much
merci infiniment	thank you very much indeed
merci mille fois	a thousand thanks
encore merci	thanks again

■ You're welcome

je vous en prie
de rien
(il n'y a) pas de quoi ⎤   you're welcome, it was nothing

c'est moi (qui vous remercie)   it's for me to thank you

■ Sorry

pardon	pardon, sorry, excuse me
excusez-moi	sorry, excuse me
pardonnez-moi (de vous avoir dérangé)	excuse me (for disturbing you)
pardon, je vous ai coupé la parole	sorry, I interrupted you
vous permettez?	may I?

■ Enjoy yourself

bonne matinée/soirée/journée	have a good morning/evening/day
bonne fin de soirée	enjoy the rest of your evening
bonne fin de semaine	have a good weekend
bon weekend	
bon après-midi	have an enjoyable afternoon (not *good afternoon*, which is translated by **bonjour**)
bonnes vacances	happy holidays
amusez-vous bien	enjoy yourself
bon appétit	enjoy your meal

In French you can put **bon/bonne** in front of pretty well anything with the sense of wishing someone a good time while they're doing it: **bon concert, bonne continuation,** even **bon travail.**

■ You too

et vous de même
et vous aussi
à vous pareillement ⎤   and the same to you

■ Goodbye

au revoir	goodbye
salut	bye, cheerio
ciao	ciao
à la prochaine	see you
à tout de suite	see you very shortly (e.g. 10 minutes)
à tout à l'heure	see you soon (e.g. in a couple of hours)
à demain/mardi	see you tomorrow/Tuesday
à un de ces jours	see you again sometime
au plaisir (de vous revoir)	till we meet again

Contractions and slang

Informal French is characterised by the use of contractions, a selection of which are given below. It is never necessary to use these colloquial variants, indeed they are frequently ungrammatical, but they are very much a part of real French.

Most are designed to make things easier to say, but some are sloppier than others. Those marked with an asterisk should be used only in very relaxed speech.

■ Contractions

cela	ça
tu	t' *
il y a	y'a *
peut-être a-t-il/ont-ils/*etc*	p'tet qu'il a/qu'ils ont/*etc*
quelle heure est-il...	quelle heure il est?
où est-il/elle/*etc*	où il/elle/*etc* est?
bien	ben
celui-là	çui-là
je ne sais pas	je sais pas, j'sais pas, shay pas
écologiste *mf & adj*	écolo
apéritif *m*	apéro
cinéma *m*	ciné, cinoche
dictionnaire *m*	dico
dissertation *f*	dissert
examen *m*	exam
extraordinaire	extra
faculté, université *f*	fac
fasciste *mf & adj*	facho
imperméable *m*	imper
intellectuel(le) *m/f*	intello
interrogation *f*	interro
manifestation *f*	manif
périphérique *m* (ringroad)	périf
petit déjeuner *m*	p'tit dej
professeur *m*	prof
réfectoire *m* (dining hall)	réf
restaurant *m*	resto
restaurant universitaire *m*	ru
télévision *f*	télé, téloche
valise *f*	valoche

Another characteristic of colloquial speech is the liking for slang substitutes for common words. What follows is a selection of the most frequently used slang.

■ People

baba(-cool) *mf & adj*	hippy
BCBG *mf & adj*	Sloane; preppy (US)
copain *m*	friend, boyfriend
copine *f*	friend, girlfriend
faux jeton *m*	dodgy bloke
frangin *m*	brother
frangine *f*	sister
gars *m*	boy
glandeur *m*	lazy devil
gringalet *m*	runt, weed
grosse légume *f*	bigwig
larve *f*	wimp
machin(e) *m/f*	thingy (e.g. **t'as vu machin?**)
mec *m*	bloke
also **type** *m*	
mémé *m*	granny; old dear
minet(te) *m/f*	fashion-conscious young man/woman, trendy
nana *f*	girl
also **mef** *f*	
pépé *m*	granddad; old chap
pif *m*	nose
also **tarin** *m*	
plouc *m*	hick, redneck
pote *m*	mate, chum
sale gosse *m*	little brat
tire-au-flanc *m*	skiver
tombeur *m*	ladies' man, lady-killer
tronche *f*	face
also **bouille** *f*	
zonard *m*	dropout

The adjectives below can also be used as substantives, e.g. **ce sont tous des coincés**:

branché	trendy
cinglé	mad, nuts
also **fêlé, maboul, toqué**	

coincé	inhibited, set in one's ways
dur	tough
minable	pathetic, hopeless; seedy
ringard	fuddy-duddy; corny
vache	mean, nasty

And a few colloquial verbs relating to things people do:

avoir du pot	to be lucky (so if you're unlucky **tu manques de pot**)
avoir la trouille, avoir le trac	to be afraid
craquer	to crack up (usually when people lose control or break down, though one might be overcome with pleasure - **il me fait craquer** - and anyone or anything really marvellous could be **craquant**.)
crever	to die
draguer	to chat up
être emballé par	to be keen on, get worked up about
faire un bide	to be a flop
faire une touche	to be a hit
ficher	to do cf. **fichez-moi la paix,** get out, clear off
gueuler	to shout, yell
mater	to stare at
mettre les voiles	to leave
piger	to understand e.g. **tu piges?**, do you get it?
poser un lapin à qn	to stand s.o. up
prendre son pied	to enjoy oneself
rigoler	to laugh, have fun
roupiller	to sleep
regagner ses pénates	to go home
se marrer	to have fun
se taper	to have e.g. **on s'est tapé une soupe à l'oignon**

■ Food and drink

avoir la dalle	to be hungry
becquetance *f*	food, grub
becqueter bouffer	eat
caler à table	to be full
casser la croûte	to have something to eat
flotte *f*	water (**flotter** is *to rain* in colloquial French)
gavé	full-up
gueleton *m*	nosh-up
picrate *m*	cheap red wine (**"le bon rouge qui tache!"**)
pinard *m*	wine

■ School and work

bahut *m*	school
bête *f*	genius e.g. **c'est une vraie bête en maths,** s/he's brilliant at maths
bosser	to work
bosseur, -euse	hard worker
boulot *m*	job, work **"Métro-boulot-dodo"** was a formula coined to describe the joyless routine of the Parisian commuter. **Faire dodo** is a child's word for **dormir.**
bouquin *m*	book
chouchou *f*	favourite
galérer	to suffer, endure (in a horrible job) **une galère** is any kind of awful job or wretched situation: **quelle galère!**
peinard	cushy (i.e. of a job. Also **on est peinard ici,** *it's good here* or *we really have it easy here*
piston *m*	pulling strings so: **avoir du piston,** *to have friends in high places*
pistonner qn	to pull strings for someone
planque *f*	cushy job
c'est la planque!	it's a doss!

se planter	to come a cropper
je me suis planté à l'examen	I failed the exam
	cf. **se planter en voiture**, *to have a car accident*
sécher des cours	to skip classes

■ Things

bagnole *f*	car
also **caisse** *f*	
baraque *f*	house
bled, trou *m*	(dead-and-alive) hole
camelote *f*	shoddy goods, junk
canard *m*	newspaper, rag
clope *f*	cigarette
also **sèche** *f*	
fric *m*	money, dosh
also **blé** *m*	
godasses *fpl*	shoes
machin, truc *m*	thing, whatsit
mauvais plan *m*	bad/boring idea
navet *m*	flop
plumard *m*	bed
tube *m*	hit (e.g. pop song)

Things - and even people - could be described as:

à la manque	second-rate, half-baked
bidon	third-rate, tacky
canon	great
	e.g. **une fille canon**, *a gorgeous girl*; **une idée canon**, *a great idea*
chouette	great
cool	informal
craignos	dodgy; stupid; corny
dégueulasse	disgusting
dément, démentiel	wild, mad
dingue	crazy
flippant	fasntastic
foireux	lousy e.g. un plan foireux
génial	super
moche	rotten, awful; ugly

nul	lousy
rasoir, rasant	boring
relax	relaxed
super	fantastic
terrible	terrific

Vachement, archi and **hyper** operate as intensifiers: **c'est vachement chouette, c'était hyper-flippant, la salle était archipleine.**

Finally a few common formulaic expressions:

je m'en fiche	
(j'en ai) rien à faire	I don't care
(j'en ai) ras-le-bol	
j'en ai marre	I'm sick of it
also **y'en a marre**	
il faut que je fonce	I've got to hurry
on se grouille	we're off, lets go
also **on se magne**	
on se casse	
on se barre	
on se tire	
on fout le camp	

Bad language

If you are invited to dinner in the **seizième** (the poshest of the Paris **arrondissements**) here is a list of expressions best avoided. No single French swear word has quite the impact of the four-letter word in English; rather, offense is given by an accumulation of **grossièretés**, e.g. **putain de merde!**. An authentic accent and delivery are also crucial.

Generally it may be wiser to learn to understand the strongest expletives, rather than to use them. But then we're all human!

■ Blast! - *mild expletives*

(ah bin) mince ⎤	oh dear, blow it
zut ⎦	
merde	drat
nom d'un chien	blimey
oh/ah la vache/les vaches	blimey, damn; the swine(s)/pig(s)
bon sang ⎤	good Lord
mon Dieu ⎦	
juste ciel	good heavens
à Dieu ne plaise	God forbid
ma foi	well, really
tais-toi	be quiet, shut up
tonnerre de Dieu	hell and damnation
tonnerre (de Brest)	by thunder, ye Gods
fichtre	gosh
allez oust	get out (of here), buzz off

■ @#~*!!! - *Strong expletives*

putain	shit!, fuck!
also **putain de merde**	
merde de merde	
bordel de merde	
bon Dieu	

Alors may follow the above, e.g. **merde alors!**

■ Le cul

– which, as well as meaning *arse*, is an effective slang translation of *sex*. Hence **histoires de cul** – *smutty stories* – and **film du cul** – *porn film*.

baiser	to fuck
also **sauter, tringler**	
bite *f*	cock
chatte *f*	cunt
couilles *fpl*	balls
derche *f*	arse
enculer	to bugger
tailler une pipe à qn	to give someone a blow job
gouine *f*	lesbian
pédé *m*	queer, fag
also **pédale** *f*, **tante** *f*	
peloter	to fondle
pute *f*	prostitute
s'envoyer en l'air	to have it off; to come
travelo *m*	queer, fag; transvestite

■ Giving offense

A man can be referred to abusively as **un con**, **un connard**, **un enculé** or **un salaud**, all of which could translate as *bastard* or *cunt*. For a woman, offensive equivalents of *bitch* or *cow* include **salope**, **garce** and **connasse**.

In every case, the effect is heightened by adding the adjective **sale** ("**sale con**") or **espèce de** ("**espèce d'enculé**").

The standard repertoire of offensive language also includes the following items. The same language elements - **con, foutre, merde** etc. - have been central to coarse French for centuries.

baiser

les baiseurs et les baisés	the ones who do the shitting and the ones who get shat on
on est baisé	we're fucked; we've had it

chier

chier	to shit
tu me fais chier	you make me sick
je l'ai envoyé chier	I told him to bugger off
c'est chiant	it's crap; it's a pain in the arse
c'était (nul) à chier	it was bloody awful
quelle chierie!	what a bloody mess!
les chiottes *f pl*	the bog, the john

con

con *adj*	bloody stupid
des conneries	rubbish, bullshit
déconner	to (talk) bullshit; to fool around
sans déconner!	no joking!, no shit!

cul

on se magne le cul	we're off; let's go
j'en ai ras le cul	I've had it up to here
il a du cul, celui-là	he's a lucky sod
ils enculent des mouches	they're nit-picking

foutre

fous le camp	piss off
va te faire foutre	go fuck yourself
c'est foutu	we've had it, it's fucked
qu'est-ce que tu fous?	what the hell are you doing?
tu l'as foutu où?	where the hell did you put it?
je m'en fous	I don't give a fuck
ce que j'en ai à foutre	what a fucking nightmare
se foutre dedans	to put one's foot in it
il se fout de nos gueules	he's taking the piss out of us
rien à foutre	no way, not bloody likely
foutrement	bloody, fucking

merde

être dans la merde also se foutre dans la merde	to be up shit creek, be in the shit
merdique	shitty; pathetic
la démerde	smooth talk
se démerder	to get by, manage
un démerdeur	bullshitter, smooth-talker
emmerder	to annoy
je m'emmerde	I'm bored stiff
emmerdant	annoying; boring
un emmerdeur/ une emmerdeuse	a pain in the arse

PART
2

PART

2

Nouns with difficult genders

Try putting a gender to these nouns:

apogée	araignée
eau	gorille
cimetière	chaumière
magazine	médecine
tête-à-tête	portefeuille
été	bonheur
vodka	après-midi

Answers can be checked against the following lists of nouns which tend to produce gender mistakes.

■ Masculine nouns

abîme	abyss
ange	angel
anniversaire	birthday
antidote	antidote
apogée	peak
article	article
artifice	artifice
asile	asylum, home, refuge
atome	atom
automne	autumn
avion	aeroplane
baptême	baptism
beurre	butter
bidonville	shanty town
blâme	blame
bonheur	happiness
buste	bust
café	cafe, coffee
caniche	poodle
caprice	whim, fancy
caractère	character
centre	centre
chapitre	chapter
charme	charm

71

choix	choice
chou-fleur	cauliflower
cimetière	cemetery
code	code
commentaire	commentary
commerce	trade
conte	story
contexte	context
contraire	contrary
contraste	contrast
contrôle	control
cosmétique	hair oil
crépuscule	dusk, twilight
crime	crime
cycle	cycle, bicycle
derrière	backside, behind, rear
dialecte	dialect
dialogue	dialogue
dilemme	dilemma
diplôme	diploma, exam
disque	record
dogme	dogma
domaine	domain, field
domicile	home, address
doute	doubt
échange	exchange
élastique	elastic band
éloge	praise
épisode	episode
équilibre	balance
espace	space
été	summer
exemple	example
exercice	exercise
fleuve	river
folklore	folklore
génie	genius, genie; engineering
geste	gesture
globule	corpuscle
grade	rank, grade

groupe	group
guide	guide
gymnase	gymnasium
honneur	honour
incendie	fire
indice	index, indication, clue
insecte	insect
intervalle	interval
jade	jade
laboratoire	laboratory
légume	vegetable
linge	linen, washing
liquide	liquid
losange	diamond
luxe	luxury
lycée	lycée (French secondary school)
magazine	magazine
malaise	feeling of faintness, unrest, malaise
malheur	misfortune
manque	lack, shortage, shortcoming
massacre	massacre
masque	mask
mélange	mixture
mensonge	lie
mérite	merit
mime	mime
minuit	midnight
miracle	miracle
mode	method, way
modèle	model
monopole	monopoly
moustique	mosquito
murmure	murmur
musée	museum
ongle	nail, claw
orchestre	orchestra
ordre	order
Pacifique	Pacific
pacte	pact

pamplemousse	grapefruit
parachute	parachute
paragraphe	paragraph
parapluie	umbrella
pastiche	pastiche
pétale	petal
pétrole	(crude) oil, parafin
peuple	people
phénomène	phenomenon
pique-nique	picnic
poème	poem
pore	pore
portefeuille	wallet, portfolio
pouce	thumb; inch
pourboire	tip
problème	problem
programme	programme
refuge	refuge
Reine Elisabeth	Queen Elizabeth (ship)
renne	reindeer
reproche	reproach
reste	rest
rêve	dream
rhume	cold
rire	laugh
risque	risk
rôle	role
rythme	rhythm
sable	sand
sacrifice	sacrifice
salaire	salary
satellite	satellite
scandale	scandal
siècle	century
signe	sign
silence	silence
souffle	breath
squelette	skeleton
stade	stage, stadium
sucre	sugar
suicide	suicide

suspense	suspense
symbole	symbol
système	system
téléphone	telephone
terme	term
territoire	territory
tête-à-tête	tête-à-tête
texte	text
thé	tea
théâtre	theatre
timbre	stamp, timber
tonnerre	thunder
trimestre	term, quarter
triomphe	triumph
trophée	trophy
uniforme	uniform
vaudeville	vaudeville
ventre	stomach, belly
verbe	verb
vestibule	hall
vice	vice
vide	vacuum, emptiness
vocabulaire	vocabulary
volume	volume
vote	vote
zèle	zeal

Nouns denominating professions remain masculine even when referring to a woman, though **femme** can be added in all the following cases (e.g. **femme architecte**):

architecte
auteur
écrivain
facteur
médecin
ministre
peintre
professeur
sculpteur

■ Feminine nouns

atmosphère	atmosphere
bande-annonce	movie trailer
bibliothèque	library
cage	cage
chanson	song
clef/clé	key
communauté	community
cour	court(-yard)
croix	cross
cuiller	spoon
cuisson	cooking
dent	tooth
difficulté	difficulty
eau	water
énigme	enigma
espèce	species, sort (see also *Contractions and Slang*)
fin	end
foi	faith
fois	time
forêt	forest
fourmi	ant
image	picture, image
interview	interview
liqueur	liqueur
loi	law
mi-mai (etc...)	middle of May (etc...)
mi-temps	half-time
oasis	oasis
page	page
paix	peace
paroi	wall
peau	skin
plage	beach
prison	prison
radio	radio
rage	rage; rabies

rançon	ransom
syllabe	syllable
toux	cough
vertu	virtue
villa	villa (i.e. by the sea)
vis	screw
vodka	vodka

Some feminine nouns remain feminine even when denoting a man:

connaissance	acquaintance
personne	person
vedette	star
victime	victim
star	star

Note these special cases:

1. **amour** is masculine in the singular but most often feminine in the plural. It is sometimes encountered in literature as a masculine plural. When it means *cupid* or *cherub* (e.g. in a painting) the plural is masculine.

2. **délice** is masculine in the singular and feminine in the plural.

3. **orgue** is masculine in the singular. When used in the plural to denote a single instrument (e.g. a big organ in a church: **les grandes orgues**) it is feminine. However two or more distinct instuments would be referred to in the masculine plural, e.g. **les deux orgues sont fort différents**.

4. **Pâques** meaning *Easter* is masculine singular, despite the **s**. It is feminine plural when accompanied by an adjective, e.g. **bonnes Pâques**. Note however **à Pâques prochain**.

The gender of several nouns differs according to meaning. The most important are listed in the *Distinctions* section on page 79.

Tricky spellings

Some French spellings are tricky because they differ slightly from a similar word in English, e.g. **adresse**. Others are just plain difficult.

☆ Before you look through these lists, how would you spell the French for

marriage
reflection
religion
perfectionist

adresse *f*	address
aigu, aiguë	sharp, acute
agression *f*	aggression
alternative *f*	alternative
américain	American
apparemment	apparently
appartement *m*	flat, apartment
ça et là	here and there
céder	yield
description	description
épisode *m*	episode
en général	in general
extrémisme *m*	extremism
Grèce *f*	Greece
grec, grecque	Greek
galerie *f*	gallery
mariage *m*	marriage
Maroc	Morocco
perfectionniste	perfectionist
récompenser	to reward
réflexion *f*	reflection
religion *f*	religion
répondre	answer
répéter	repeat
rythme *m*	rhythm
sélection *f*	selection
symétrie *f*	symmetry
vérité *f*	truth

Distinctions

Distinguish carefully between the words in these groups. Some of them sound the same (homophones), look the same (homonyms) or are misleadingly similar to English words.

■ Homophones and homonyms

la chaire	pulpit, chair (i.e. professorship)
la chair	flesh
le champagne	champagne
la Champagne	Champagne (the region)
le chèvre	goat's-milk cheese
la chèvre	goat
le crêpe	crepe
la crêpe	pancake
le critique	critic
la critique	criticism, review; the critics
la foi	faith
le foie	liver
la forêt	forest
le foret	drill
le poêle	stove
la poêle	frying pan
le livre	book
la livre	pound
le manche	handle
la manche	sleeve
la Manche	Channel
le mode	method, way
la mode	fashion
le dessin	drawing
le dessein	intention
le pair	peer, equal
la paire	pair
la poire	pear

le tour	tour; trick
la tour	tower
la vapeur	steam, vapour
le vapeur	steamer
le vase	vase
la vase	mud, silt
le voile	veil
la voile	sail

■ Faux amis

Similarity to English can lead to mistranslation in the following cases:

le parasol	(large/table) parasol
une ombrelle	(handheld) parasol
un argument	argument (i.e. case)
la dispute	argument (between people), dispute
la figure	face
le chiffre	figure
le cargo	cargo boat
la cargaison	cargo, load
le flegme	composure, phlegm
la flemme	laziness
séculaire	age-old
séculier	secular
par hasard	by chance
au hasard	haphazardly, at random, off the top of one's head
l'ingénuité	ingenuousness
l'ingéniosité	ingenuity
disgracieux	awkward, unsightly
honteux	disgraceful
malicieux	mischievous
malveillant	malicious
soupçonneux	suspicious (i.e. suspecting)
louche	suspicious (i.e. appears suspicious)

abusif	improper, unauthorised
injurieux	abusive
une étable	cowshed
une écurie	stable
officiellement	officially
officieusement	unofficially
une part de gâteau	slice of cake
une tranche de pain	slice of bread
une rondelle de carotte	slice of carrot
le coquillage	shellfish
la coque	hull, body, fuselage; cockle
la coquille	shell, scallop; misprint
la sueur	sweat
la suie	soot
une saucisse	(small) sausage
un saucisson	(slicing) sausage
la défiance	distrust
le défi	defiance
compréhensif	understanding
complet	comprehensive
la pétrole	oil
l'essence *f*	petrol

Translation notes

■ English into French

The first problem of translating a passage from English into French is that working from the English may encourage you to use English structures in French, where they can be inappropriate. You should therefore consciously focus on writing French which you know to be correct from experience. The difficulty which remains is to do this without losing any of the subtlety of the original.

Clarifying the English is often the route to the correct French translation:

a six year old boy with grey trousers = **un garçon de six ans qui porte un pantalon gris** (Not **avec**).

He loved those around him. = **Il aimait ceux qui l'entouraient.** (Not **autour de lui**).

He face became dark. = **Son visage s'obscurcit.** (Not **devînt obscur**).

These examples demonstrate the necessity of avoiding the tendency, sometimes subconscious, towards literalness. The same problem exists in translating out of French, though it should of course be easier to spot bad English, based too literally on the French.

Checking for careless errors is the second major consideration:

l'adresse (not **addresse**)
dangereux (not **dangéreux**)
regarder de près (not **de prêt**)
la vraie morale (not **vrai**)
il l'a tuée (her) (not **tué**)

Even if you are very thorough, it is wise to check your final version at least twice. If you find yourself dwelling on a point of difficulty, move on and return to it later.

■ French into English

One of the most important things to keep in mind when translating a passage into English is that, however complex the French may appear, it means something which is clear and intelligible. The first stage of translation is to understand this meaning in all its subtlety. Words which are unknown can be guessed by studying their context or by analysing their constituent parts. For example, consider the noun **l'assolement.** If we know **sous-sol** is a basement, we may associate **sol** with ground and thus infer the meaning *putting to ground* which in the context may lead to the correct meaning: *planting*.

The second and final stage is putting the "decoded" text into good English. The aim must always be to make the English sound completely convincing. In addition, try to avoid words which obviously correspond with their French equivalents; spend just a little more time finding a richer synonym.

It is usually best to read through the entire passage briskly first of all, in order to give yourself the benefit of the whole context and so facilitate comprehension. Then "decode" it, writing down your first version, which is accurate in meaning, but poor in English style. And finally write the passage in convincing English. If stuck on a word, do not dwell on it but return to it later. In checking, take care that you have not omitted to translate parts of the passage or missed small points of detail.

Translation practice - description

These sentence examples, mostly descriptive in nature, are chosen to highlight some tricks of the translator's trade. Try translating them yourself before you look at the French. Pay particular attention to the use of reflexive verbs.

There is a very tall building in the middle of the town.
Un bâtiment se dresse/s'élève très haut au milieu de la ville.

There was a low-lying layer of dirty grey clouds.
Il y avait une couche basse de nuages gris sale.

A veil of mist is forming in the hollows of the hills.
Un voile de brume se forme dans les creux des collines.

The road stretched away before them.
La route s'allongeait devant eux.

The path opens on to the road.
Le sentier débouche sur la route.

The window looks on to the garden.
La fenêtre s'ouvre/donne sur le jardin.

I turned on to the road/into the street.
J'ai débouché sur la route/dans la rue.

We passed the farm.
Nous passâmes devant la ferme.

It is 60 kilometres/an hour from London.
C'est à 60 kilomètres/une heure de Londres.

You can make out a river.
On devine un fleuve.

The window-panes are misting up.
Les vitres s'embuent.

She stayed quite motionless.
Elle demeurait tout immobile.

He is broad-shouldered.
Il a une bonne carrure.

There was a hint of sadness about him.
Il avait un je ne sais quoi de mélancolique.

I opened my eyes wide.
J'ouvris grand mes yeux.

It's a town which has a strange character.
C'est une ville qui revêt un caractère bizarre.

She was chilled with a sense of foreboding.
Un pressentiment lui glaçait l'esprit.

He was a man of remarkable intellect.
C'était un homme d'une intelligence remarquable.

He spoke in a faint voice, interspersed with sobs.
Il parlait d'une voix faible où affleuraient des sanglots.

She gulped down three brandies.
Elle a sifflé trois cognacs.

He shuddered.
Il eut un frisson.

Essays and journalism

The ability to express oneself at length in written French without grammatical errors is clearly a major asset. When writing an essay for an exam, there are two principal aspects to consider: first, what one may call the march of the argument and second, the correctness of the French.

One may be asked to write about either a subject (e.g. **L'énergie nucléaire**) or a quotation (e.g. **L'enfer c'est les autres**). When writing about a quotation it is important to acknowledge all that it may be referring to and to analyse any in-built assumptions it may have. Before beginning to write, it is vital to be able to think fairly precisely what you want to say and what examples you want to use. You should already have in mind the conclusion you wish to reach before starting to write.

If an essay plan takes longer than ten minutes, it is either too detailed (one need only list examples) or should be dropped in favour of another subject because the one chosen is presenting you with too much difficulty. By having a clear idea of the conclusion, you can concentrate on ensuring that the examples chosen and the way in which they are presented lead logically to it.

At the start of the essay, it is important to define your terms, in other words, to say how you interpret the meaning of the subject and what elements of it you are going to limit yourself to discussing. You can then go on to the consideration of various examples. It may be appropriate to include the historical background as well as contemporary incidents. It is also a good idea to draw from your own personal experience to illustrate points. Each example should take the march of the argument a step forward. Your conclusion - which is the true heart of an essay - will benefit if you have given equal attention to the best points of opposing views, impartially describing how these views have come to be held. Only when you come to the conclusion, should you allow yourself space to make an opinion, based on what has been deduced from the body of the essay. The subject may then be set in perspective with an allusion to wider implications.

Writing correct French is easier in an essay than a translation from English because you have the freedom to say what you want to say. It follows that you should only use French which you know is correct. Try not, even subconsciously, to make ambitious, literal or semi-literal translations of complex English. Instead, keep the French straightforward and embellish it with stock phrases where appropriate. Write on alternate lines so that you have space to make corrections. Then reread it meticulously, checking for careless errors, such as the omission of accents and wrong adjectival agreements.

The following expressions and phrases have been chosen for their usefulness in essays, journalism and any type of argued prose.

il y a du pour et du contre
there are reasons for and against

j'indique, pour que les idées soient claires, que...
to clarify matters, I should like to point out that...

mais qui pourra y porter remède?
but who will be able to come up with a solution?

l'histoire aurait pu se terminer là
the story could have ended there

le problème reste donc entier
and so the problem remains

ce problème ne comporte pas de solution facile
this problem does not have an easy solution

cette citation présente un grand intérêt/résume un grave problème
this quotation is particularly interesting/broaches a serious problem

sur quoi cette déclaration se fonde-t-elle?
on what is this statement based?

il n'empêche que cette politique sera bien entendu poursuivie
this policy will of course be carried out all the same

il a, sans doute, tenu pour plus grave encore que...
he has doubtless seen it as even more serious that...

cela pousse à la consommation
this leads to increased consumption

il se rabattent sur d'autres moyens
they are falling back on other means

d'après les bruits qui courent...
rumour has it that...

ils mettent au point une nouvelle coopération militaire avec ce pays
they are arranging new military cooperation with this country

cela a suscité de grandes espérances
this has raised great hopes

cela a levé, en grande partie, nos inquiétudes
this has largely dispelled our worries

mais il y a pire
but there is worse to come

ils ont mis au pas les groupements extrémistes
they have kept the extremist groups in check

elle a pris des mesures à l'encontre de son rival
she took measures against her rival

cela n'a plus sa place sur la scène politique
this no longer has a place on the political scene

ils font de cette question le principal cheval de bataille de leur propagande
they make this question the hobby-horse of their propaganda

la situation est très perturbée
the situation is very serious

ils ont été mis en présence des conditions
they were shown the conditions

cela nous fournit au moins un bouche-trou
it at least provided us with a stop-gap

ils avaient raison de sonner le tocsin
they were right to sound the alarm

c'est plus important qu'on ne le pense
it is more important than you would think

c'est un des points chauds de l'actualité
it is one of today's burning issues

il foule ses principes aux pieds
he is trampling his principles underfoot

en réalité, l'espionnage existe bel et bien dans notre pays
in fact, spying quite certainly goes on in our country

ils entendent appliquer beaucoup d'effort pour conserver leur aire d'influence
they intend going to great lengths to maintain their sphere of influence

cette citation comporte plusieurs interprétations
this quotation can be interpreted in several way

c'est déjà un pas pris dans la bonne direction
it's already a step in the right direction

cela constitue un éclatant désaveu de la politique du gouvernement
this amounts to a striking repudiation of the government's policy

une conclusion s'impose
one conclusion is inescapable

de ce que j'ai dit il ressort que ...
from what I have said it follows that...

cette politique va directement à l'encontre de tout ce qui est moral
this policy goes against all that is moral

pour les raisons précédemment énumérées...
for the above reasons...

pour autant que l'on puisse juger à ce stade des choses
as far as we can judge in the current situation

la campagne portera, pour l'essentiel, sur deux grands thèmes
the campaign will essentially focus on two issues

News vocabulary

aléas *mpl*	hazards, chanciness
aperçu *m*	idea (**de**, of); insight (**sur**, into)
apothéose *f*	apotheosis, zenith
appellation *f*	name, term
atonie *f*	lifelessness
avatars *mpl*	ups and downs
aubaine *f*	godsend
audio-visuel, l' *m*	television and radio (the industry)
barrage *m* **de police**	roadblock
bavure *f*	mistake, boob
bien-fondé *m*	cogency
à bout portant	point-blank (range)
à brûle-pourpoint	point-blank (request)
cadre *m*	framework; executive
carcan *m*	shackles (e.g. **le carcan familial**)
cécité *f*	blindness
changement *m* **de cap**	change of direction/course
clip *m*	music-video, film clip
condamnation *f* **à mort**	capital punishment
conférence *f* **de presse**	press conference
congrès *m*	congress, conference (e.g. academic)
côté cocorico, le	element of bravado
cotisation *f*	contribution
cours *m*	class, lecture (one of a series)
créneau *m*	gap, parking space
creuset *m*	melting pot
débrayage *m*	stoppage (strike)
décalage *m*	discrepancy, gap, interval, change
défaillance *f*	(feeling) of weakness, failing; fault, breakdown
défaut *m* **dans la cuirasse**	chink in the armour
démarche *f*	step (e.g. **une démarche prudente,** a wise step)
devis *m*	estimate, quotation
dicton *m*	saying
disette *f*	shortage
D.O.M.-T.O.M. *mpl*	overseas departments and territories
données *fpl*	facts, data
échappatoire *f*	evasion, way out

effet *m* d'ensemble	overall effect
égalité *f* des chances	equal oppotunities
égérie *f*	brains, mastermind
empreinte digitale	fingerprint
enchevêtrement *m*	tangle, confusion
engouement *m*	craze, infatuation
enjeu *m*	what is at stake
entretien *m*	interview, discussion, meeting
essor *m*	rise, rapid growth (e.g. of an industry)
exutoire *m*	outlet release
facteur *m*	factor
faire la une des journaux	to be on the front page, be headline news
flair *m*	sense of smell (dog); intuition, sixth sense
fléau *m*	scourge, curse, bane
frapper d'ostracisme	to ostracize
gaffe *f*	mistake, boob
grève *f*	strike
grève *f* de la faim	hunger strike
grève perlée	go slow
grève sauvage	wildcat strike
grève du zèle	work-to-rule
grief *m*	grievance
gros plan	close-up
guet-apens *m*	trap, ambush
Hexagone, l' *m*	(mainland) France
image *f* de marque	reputation
idée *f* maîtresse	underlying idea/theory
intempéries *fpl*	bad weather
interrogation *f*	test (e.g. at school)
interview *f*	interview (e.g. TV, radio)
lavage *m* de cerveaux	brainwashing
leurre *m*	decoy
lubie *f*	whim, fad
magma *m*	magma, muddle
mainmise *f*	seizure, (undesirable) involvement/control
manège *m*	game, ploy; merry-go-round
manifestation *f*	demonstration (i.e. protest)
marasme *m*	stagnation
média(s) *mpl*	media

médisance *f*	backbiting
mettre en oeuvre	to implement
mise en garde *f*	warning
montant *m*	total, total amount
nantis *mpl*	rich, well-to-do
optique *f*	opinion, point of view
pagaille *f*	shambles, muddle
patrimoine *m*	inheritance, heritage
perspectives *fpl*	outlook
plaidoyer *m*	plea
pléonasme *m*	tautology
point *m* de non-retour	point of no return
politique *f* de la terre brûlée	scorched earth policy
pour et le contre, le	the pros and cons
pourquoi et les comment, les	the whys and wherefores
prestation *f*	performance (e.g. in sport)
faire une bonne prestation	to perform well
profane *m*	layman, beginner
progrès *mpl*	progress
publicité *f*	advertisement, commercial (TV, radio)
question épineuse	prickly/thorny question
rapprochement *m*	bringing together
recensement *m*	census
recrudescence *f*	upsurge, outbreak
remaniement (ministériel)	(cabinet) reshuffle, revision
rendement *m*	productivity, yield, output
rivalité *f*	rivalry
rixe *f*	brawl, scuffle
rumeur *f* sans fondement	groundless rumour
siège social	head office
stage *m*	course
stagiaire *m/f*	trainee
surenchère *f*	higher bid, build-up, overstatement, outdoing
surenchère de violence	increase in violence
théorie appuyée sur les faits	theory borne out by facts
tonus *m*	energy
tournant *m*	turning point
truquer les élections	to gerrymander
tuer dans l'oeuf	to nip in the bud
ville-dortoir *f*	commuter town

Business and financial French

acquisition *f* d'une société par effet de levier, LBO — LBO, leveraged buy-out

actif *m* — assets

action *f* — share (i.e. equity)

agent *m* de change — stockbroker

augmenter de — increase by

B(N)PA = Bénéfice *m* par action — earnings per share

baisser de — fall by

bilan *m* — balance-sheet

Bourse *f* — Paris Stock Exchange

branche *f* — division

cadre *m* — executive

CAHT= Chiffre d'Affaires Hors Taxe — turnover

capitale boursière *f* — market capitalisation

CFPA= CashFlow par Action — cashflow per share

charges *fpl* — expenses

charges financières — financial charges

City *f* — International Stock Exchange (of London); the City

Conseil *m* d'Administration — Board of Directors

coté — quoted (i.e. on the market)

cours *m* de l'aluminium — aluminium price

courtier *m* — broker

décor *m* — financial/economic landscape

découvert *m* — overdraft

déficitaire — loss-making

dessous-de-table *mpl* — backhandlers (literally: under the table)

durcissement de la concurrence — tougher competition

à grande échelle — large-scale

entreprise *f* — company

exercice *m* financier — financial year

Fed *f* — the Fed (US Federal Investment Board)

filiale *f* — subsidiary

fonds *mpl* propres — shareholders' funds

frais *mpl*	fees
fusion *f*	merger
fusionner	merge
gérant *m* **de fonds**	fund manager
gestion *f*	management
grosses capitalisations *fpl*	(lit: companies with large market capitalisations) blue chips
hausse *f* **du dollar/des prix pétroliers**	rise in the dollar/crude oil price
honoraires *mpl*	fees
indice *m* **Dow Jones**	Dow Jones index
injection *f* **de cash**	cash injection
institut *m* **de conjoncture économique**	financial institute
institutionnels *mpl*	institutions (i.e. insurance companies, pension funds, etc)
introduction *f* **en bourse**	flotation
limitation *f* **d'approvisionnements**	shortage of supply
marge (opérationnelle)	(operating) margin
marque *f* **déposée**	registered trademark
matières premières	raw materials
multinationale *f*	multinational
offre publique *f* **d'achat, OPA**	takeover bid
part *f*	share (of, for example, GDP), stake
passer de x à y	to rise from x to y (e.g. per cent increase)
passif *m*	liabilities
PIB= Produit *m* **Intérieur Brut**	GDP
placement *m*	investment
plus-values *fpl*	capital gains
pot-de-vin *m*	bribe (literally: jug of wine)
Président-Directeur Général, PDG *m*	managing director, chairman, chief executive director, CED
premier semestre *m*	first half (i.e. first six months
profitable	profitable
rachat *m* **d'entreprise par les salariés**	MBO, management buy-out

rapport *m*	link, rapport; report, study
rapport annuel	report and accounts
rapport *m* cours-bénéfice	P/E = price/earnings ratio
récession *f*	recession
reçu *m*	receipt
recul *m*	decline, fall (e.g. in Gross Domestic Product)
résultat d'exloitation *m*	operating profit
réunion *f*	meeting
redressement *m* (du cours)	recovery (in the price)
rentable	financially viable
profitable	profitable
rentrée *f* de fonds	inflow of funds
restructurations *fpl*	restructuring
RN=Revenu Net	net profit
sans but lucratif	non-profit-making
se déprécier	depreciate
s'élever à	be/stand at (i.e. profits, interest rates)
s'endetter	get into debt
s'inscrire à	increase by
se répercuter sur	affect
siège *m* social	head-office
société *f*	company
survaleur *f*	goodwill
taux *m* d'endettement	gearing
titre *m*	stock, share
valeur *f* nette de l'actif	net asset value, NAV

Letters

A business letter is headed **Monsieur, Madame, Cher Monsieur** or **Chère Madame.** The phrase with which one signs off is more elaborate:

■ Business

veuillez agréer, Monsieur/Madame, l'assurance de mes sentiments les plus distingués

veuillez agréer nos salutations distinguées

je vous présente, Monsieur/Madame, mes plus sincères salutations

veuillez croire, Monsieur/Madame, en nos salutations les meilleures

Yours faithfully/sincerely

dans l'attente de vous lire à ce sujet, par retour, recevez, Monsieur/ Madame, nos salutations les meilleures/plus distinguées...

In anticipation of hearing from you by return, Yours faithfully...

dans l'attente de notre rencontre prochaine, soyez assuré de notre entier dévouement...

I look forward to our next meeting, Yours sincerely/ faithfully...

dans l'attente de votre réponse, veuillez recevoir, Cher Monsieur/ Chère Madame, l'expression de nos meilleurs sentiments. Bien sincèrement...

I look forward to hearing from you, Yours sincerely...

nous vous remercions de répondre rapidement et vous prions de croire, Monsieur/Madame, en l'assurance de nos sincères salutations

We thank you for your early reply, Yours faithfully/sincerely...

■ Friends and relatives

j'espère avoir bientôt de tes nouvelles	I hope to hear from you soon
meilleurs voeux bien sincèrement amicalement (ton/votre...)	best wishes, yours
en espérant que tu te portes/ vous vous portez à merveille, je t'adresse/vous adresse mes plus sincères amitiés/amicales pensées	hoping that you are in the best of health, Yours (sincerely)...
bons baisers gros becs grosses bises gros bisous	love and kisses
je t'embrasse, ton...	love

Proverbs

Some proverbs translate practically word for word, e.g. **mieux vaut tard que jamais**. In other cases French has found quite different images: **un tiens vaut mieux que deux tu l'auras.**

☆ Do you know the French equivalent of these proverbs:

> *practice makes perfect*
> *let sleeping dogs lie*
> *every cloud has a silver lining*

nécessité fait loi
needs must when the devil drives

nécessité est mère d'invention
necessity is the mother of invention

hâtez-vous lentement
more haste, less speed

c'est en forgeant qu'on devient forgeron
practice makes perfect

quand le vin est tiré, il faut le boire
what you've started you must finish

chien qui aboie ne mord pas
his bark is worse than his bite

mieux vaut tard que jamais
better late than never

n'éveille pas le chat qui dort
let sleeping dogs lie

le premier arrivé est le premier servi
first come, first served

vouloir c'est pouvoir
where there's a will, there's a way

l'habit ne fait pas le moine
don't judge a book by its cover

dans le royaume des aveugles le borgne est roi
in the kingdom of the blind the one-eyed man is king

tout ce qui brille n'est pas or
all that glitters is not gold

à bon chat bon rat
tit for tat

qui se ressemble s'assemble
birds of a feather flock together

on apprend à tout âge
you live and learn

la nuit porte conseil
sleep on it

plaie d'argent n'est pas mortelle
money isn't everything

loin des yeux, loin du coeur
out of sight, out of mind

mieux vaut prévenir que guérir
prevention is better than cure

il ne faut pas vendre la peau de l'ours avant de l'avoir tué
don't count your chickens before they're hatched

après la pluie, le beau temps
every cloud has a silver lining

un tiens vaut mieux que deux tu l'auras
a bird in the hand is worth two in the bush

Grammar

What follows is a trouble-shooting guide, focusing on key areas of difficulty.

■ Adjective agreement and positioning

Adjectives precede the noun when the adjective is considered an intrinsic part of the noun:

votre aimable mère,	*your kind mother*
le souverain pontife,	*the Pope*

When two adjectives qualify a noun, they can both follow the noun, linked by **et** or, preferably, precede and follow it:

le premier et très bon film de ...
quelque hostile bête fauve

An adjective qualifying a compound noun never interrupts the compound:

une tache de sang historique, *an historic bloodstain*

Some adjectives can be regarded as adverbs and do not agree:

la pluie tombe dru,	*the rain is falling heavily*
ils sont loin de le faire (not **loins**)	*they are far from doing it*

Note the following agreement for **gens**: feminine adj. + **gens** + masculine adj.

ces vieilles gens maladroits *those clumsy old people*

Qualified adjectives of colour remain invariable:

une rivière gris terne

This is because they were originally nouns (**une rivière d'un gris terne**) but the **d'un** is now omitted.

A few other adjectives, often of relatively recent foreign origin, are also invariable:

kaki, rococo, chic

Avoir l'air - *to look like* - should logically not lead to agreement of its qualifying adjective but **elles ont l'air content** or **contentes** are both possible, the latter being perhaps more common.

■ Articles

Notice how in these phrases French requires an article whilst English does not:

l'un des deux	*one of them (i.e. of two)*
l'un(e) ou l'autre	*one or (the) other*
ni l'un ni l'autre	*neither one nor the other*
j'y vais le samedi	*I go there on Saturdays* (cf. **j'y vais samedi,** *I'm going there on Saturday;* **j'y vais tous les samedis,** *I go there every Saturday*)
j'ai approuvé de la tête	*I nodded approval*
le sens de la justice	*sense of justice*
les paramètres du jugement	*the parameters of judgement*
le Ministre des Finances	*the Ministry of Finance*
au sud de la France	*in the south of France*
dans le Midi/Surrey/Mississippi	*in the Midi/Surrey/Mississippi*
la liberté de l'Europe	*the freedom of Europe*
le Prince Rainier	*Prince Rainier*
la Jacqueline (colloquial)	*our Jacqueline*
le jardin du Luxembourg	*Luxembourg gardens*

Here in contrast, no article is required in French:

elle est rudement jolie fille	*she is a really pretty girl*
en tant que journaliste	*as a journalist*
avec ressentiment	*resentfully*
avec vaillance	*valiantly, boldly*
avoir bonne/mauvaise réputation	*have a good/bad reputation*
cela signifie justice, égalité	*this means justice and equality*
une question de réalité	*a matter of reality*
et autres hérésies	*and other heresies*
les poissons d'eau douce	*fresh-water fish*
en Bretagne	*in Brittany*
importé de Californie	*imported from California*
les vins d'Espagne	*wines of Spain*
le roi d'Angleterre	*the King of England*

■ Comparatives and superlatives of *bon, mauvais, bien, mal*

The comparative and superlative forms of the adjectives **bon** and **mauvais** are as follows:

meilleur/plus mauvais, pire	*better/worse*
le meilleur/le plus mauvais, le pire	*the best, the worst*

Compare these with the adverbs **bien** and **mal**

mieux/pis	*better/worse*
le mieux/le pis	*he best/the worst*

Pire and **le pire** are much less common in spoken French than **plus mauvais** and **le plus mauvais**. They also tend to refer to abstract nouns, e.g. **le pire échec.** On the other hand you would speak only of **le plus mauvais fromage**, not **le pire fromage**.

In theory the two expressions are interchangeable, but **(le) pire** is uncommon in spoken French.

Pis can also be used to replace **plus mal** or **plus mauvais**:

cela va de mal en pis

It also occurs in a few set phrases, e.g.

tant pis	*too bad*
qui pis est	*what is worst*
au pis-aller	*if the worst comes to the worst*

Le pis is only used in literary French.

The forms **moins bon** and **moins bien** are common polite alternatives for the translation of *worse*.

Ce chapeau est moins bien que l'autre.

Note also these examples

elle est meilleure	*she is better* (i.e. in some specific way)
elle est mieux	*she is better* (i.e. more attractive)
bien meilleur	*a lot better* (avoid **beaucoup**)

and a highly idiomatic use of **mieux**:

Ils criaient à qui mieux mieux.	They tried to outdo each other in their shouting.

■ Exclamation

Note the following forms:

Quel sale temps!	*What awful weather!*
Que de monde ici!	*What a lot of people there are here!*
Que/Comme c'est beau!	*How beautiful it is!*

Comme c'est remarquable!	*How remarkable!*
Combien je me suis étonné!	*How surprised I was!*
Quelle femme charmante que la concierge!	*What a charming woman the concierge is!*

These exclamatory structures require the subjunctive:

Puisse le temps nous être favorable!	*Let's hope the weather is good to us!*
Puissiez-vous réussir!	*May you succeed!*
Fasse le ciel qu'il arrive à temps!	*I hope to God he arrives in time!*
Qu'on le fasse tout de suite!	*It must be done immediately!*
Qu'il vienne!	*Let him come!*

■ For, *depuis* and *pendant*

Notice how the time preposition *for* translates in these sentences:

Il y a quatre ans que je le vois.	*I've been seeing him for four years.*
Il y avait quatre ans que je le voyais.	*I had been seeing him for four years.*
Il est absent depuis une semaine.	*He has been absent for a week.*
Il a été absent (pendant) une semaine.	*He was absent for a week.*

But

Il sera absent pour une semaine.	*He will be absent for a week.*

■ *Faire/laisser* + infinitive: getting something done etc.

The variety of English translations shows how very useful these French structures are. Note also the position of the object pronoun.

j'ai fait entrer vos associés; je les ai fait entrer	*I showed your partners in; I showed them in*
j'ai fait apporter un verre de vin par le garçon; je le lui ai fait apporter	*I got the waiter to bring a glass of wine; I got him to bring it*
je me fais faire un costume; je me le fais faire	*I am having a suit made for me; I am having it made for me*
je vous le ferai écouter	*I shall get you to listen to it* - or possibly *I will play it to you*
il vous fera m'écouter	*he will get you to listen to me*
je me fais couper les cheveux	*I'm having my hair cut*
elle nous a fait savoir qu'ils étaient arrivés	*she let us know that they had arrived*
fais voir	*show (it to) me*
il fit remarquer/observer/etc que	*he remarked/observed/etc that*

certaines rumeurs font craindre la fermeture de la banque	*certain rumours suggest that the bank may close*
c'est un homme qui se laisse servir	*he's a man who expects to be waited upon*
il va se laisser faire	*he's going to let it happen/be done (to him)*
il s'était laissé pousser une barbe en pointe	*he had grown a goatee*
elle ne se laisse pas épater	*she refuses to be impressed*

■ Measurements

Note the following variants:

la pièce a dix mètres de long/ longueur	
la pièce est longue de dix mètres	
la pièce fait dix mètres de long	*the room is ten metres long*
la pièce a une longueur de dix mètres	
la longueur de cette pièce est de dix mètres	
elle est de trois mètres plus longue que l'autre	*it is three metres longer than the other one*

■ "Must" and special uses of *devoir*

Notions of obligation and certainty provide some interesting examples of 'Real French':

elle aura mangé à midi (or elle a dû manger etc.)	*she must have eaten at lunchtime*
l'expédition doit traverser les Alpes	*the expedition will/is to cross the Alps*
la réunion devra être terminée demain	*the meeting is to finish tomorrow*
il ne doit pas être si bien payé	*he can't be that well paid*

■ Negatives

ne...pas	not
ne...plus	no longer
ne...guère	hardly
ne...jamais	never
ne...rien	not anything, nothing

This order indicates position of these negatives if they are combined, e.g.

il n'aura plus jamais rien
il n'y a plus guère que Jean au café

All follow the auxiliary in compound tenses. The other negatives (**ne...aucun/ personne/que**) follow the past participle, e.g.

je n'ai vu aucun film intéressant cet hiver

Avoid **ne...point** which is literary and somewhat archaic.

Note also the following:

nul n'est venu	*no-one came*
il n'y a aucun problème	*there isn't any problem* (not **pas aucun**)
rien de tel	*nothing of the sort*
il valait donc mieux ne toucher à rien	*so it was better not to touch anything*
elles ne prêtent pas attention à ces broutilles	*they don't pay any attention to these trifles* (not **pas d'attention**)
sans mot dire	*without saying a word*

Ne is inserted in the following structures:

je crains qu'il ne me voie	*I am frightened he will see me*
cf. **je ne crains pas qu'il me voie**	*I am not frightened that he will see me*
craignez-vous qu'il (ne) vous voie?	*are you frightened that he will see you?*
il n'est pas venu de peur qu'il n'y ait un problème	*he didn't come because he is/was afraid there would be a problem*
je ne doute/nie pas qu'il ne vienne	*I don't doubt/deny that he is coming*
doutez-vous/niez-vous qu'il ne vienne?	*do you doubt/deny that he is coming?*
j'empêche/évite qu'elle ne vienne	*I am preventing her from coming*
peu s'en faut qu'il ne prenne ma place	*he nearly took my place*
à moins que vous n'ayez une objection	*unless you have an objection*
à Dieu ne plaise!	*heaven forbid!*
n'importe	*no matter*
on le prend pour plus bête qu'il n'est	*he is regarded as more stupid than he is*
elle est plus intelligente que vous ne le pensez	*she is more intelligent than you think*
si je ne m'abuse	*if I'm not mistaken*

■ Passives

Her letters were never answered cannot be directly translated into French, because the subject becomes an indirect object in the French active form:

répondre à ses lettres   *to answer her letters*

It is necessary to say, for example:

Ses lettres ne trouvaient jamais de réponse.

Likewise, *someone could be heard whistling* is also impossible to translate by a passive in French and **on** must be used:

On entendait quelqu'un qui sifflait.

On is much more common in passive sentences than *one* in Engish:

on m'a donné deux billets,   *I was given two tickets*

The reflexive pronoun commonly occurs where the passive would be used in English:

sa suprématie ne se discute pas   *his supremacy is not disputed*
ça se mange?   *can this be eaten?*
ce livre se lit partout   *this book is being read everywhere*
un concert se donne aux Arènes   *a concert is being given at the Arena*
  demain   *tomorrow*
cela ne se fait pas   *it isn't done*

■ Prepositions

Note these examples of different prepositional usage in the two languages:

je vais sur la Côte d'Azur,   *I'm going to the Côte d'Azur*
elle se penche par la fenêtre,   *she is leaning out of the window*
choisis ce que tu veux dans le panier   *choose what you want from the basket*
il l'a mis à la poubelle,   *he put it in the dustbin*
il grimpa dans un arbre/à une échelle   *he climbed (up) a tree/ladder*
il finit par une note d'optimisme,   *he finished on a note of optimism*
la meilleure boulangerie de Nîmes,   *the best bakery in Nîmes*

de, **en**, **à** and *si* should not be omitted when their sense is repeated:

en Belgique et en France   *in Belgium and France*

Note the following prepositional usages with verbs:

goûter à qch	*to taste s.t.*
acheter qch à qqn	*to buy s.t. from s.o.*
cacher qch à qqn	*to hide s.t. from s.o.*
emprunter qch à qqn	*to borrow s.t. from s.o.*
pardonner qch à qqn	*to forgive s.o. for s.t.*
elle a demandé à vous voir	*she asked to see you*
c'est difficile à déchiffrer	*it's difficult to make out*
il est difficile de le déchiffrer	*it's difficult to make it out*

■ Present participles

The use of **en** with a present participle implies two simultaneous actions:

elle mange en écoutant la radio,   *she eats listening to the radio*

One cannot use a present participle as a complement to a verb indicating a state, but must use two verbs:

elle est chez elle et écoute la radio.

Note the following translations which involve present participles in either English or French:

ne pouvant bouger, il s'écria	*unable to move, he shouted*
amoindrissant ainsi...	*thus reducing...*
sans tenir compte	*without realising* (not **sans tenant compte**)
elle écoutait son ami qui chantait	*she listened to her friend singing*

■ Relative pronouns - *qui, que, quoi, dont, où*

Relative pronouns are:

qui who, which	**lequel** which
que who(m), which	**dont** of which, whose
quoi what	**ce qui** what
où where	**ce que** what

Note the following:

QUI -

l'homme qui parle	*the man who is speaking*
l'homme à qui je parle	*the man I am talking to*

QUE -

Que is most of the time used as a direct object

la pomme que j'ai mangée était délicieuse	*the apple that I ate was delicious*
j'aime beaucoup la robe que tu portes	*I like very much the dress that you are wearing*

QUOI -

il a dit que j'avais tort, à quoi j'ai répondu qu'il se trompait	*he said I was wrong, to which I replied that he was mistaken*

DONT -

When using **dont** remember that it always begins the relative clause and is followed by the subject, the verb and the predicate, in that order, whatever order the English may be:

l'homme dont le fils est malade	*the man whose son is ill*
l'homme dont je me rappelle le fils	*the man whose son I remember*
elle me présente à ses amis dont je connaissais quelques-uns	*she introduced me to her friends, some of whom I knew*

Note also the following examples:

l'homme au fils de qui je parle	*the man with whose son I am speaking*
j'ai un rosier avec les roses duquel je ferai un joli bouquet	*I have a rosebush with the roses of which I shall make a pretty bouquet*

Dont is not used in a preposition-*whose*-noun structure like the following:

j'ai un ami aux enfants duquel (or **de qui**) **nous devons beaucoup,**	*I have a friend to whose children we owe a great deal*

■ *Si -* If, whether

In spoken French, one will rather use the indicative **si c'était lui qui revenait,** *if it was him that came back.*

Note the different equivalents to **si** and *if*:

comme possédé	*as if possessed*
si on y allait à Pâques?	*what about going there for Easter?*

When used as part of an indirect question, **si** (which can then be translated by *whether*) can be followed by any tense, depending on the context:

je lui ai demandé s'il viendrait ce soir	*I asked him if he would come this evening*
je lui ai demandé s'il était déjà venu ici	*I asked him if he had already come here*

In other cases, the following tense combinations should be adhered to:

Si + present + present, e.g.

si je crie, elle vient	*if/whenever I shout, she comes*

Si + present + future, e.g.

si elle approuve, je partirai	*if she approves, I will leave*

Si + imperfect + conditional, e.g.

si elle venait, je serais content	*if she came, I would be happy*

Si + pluperfect + past conditional, e.g.

si elle était venue, j'aurais été content	*if she had come, I would have been happy*

If...and if... can be translated by **si...et que** + subjunctive:

s'il fait beau et que je puisse te téléphoner ...	*if the weather is good and I can phone you ...*

However, the indicative is also possible:

si vous vous plaisez et que vous désirez rester, n'hésitez surtout pas	*if you like it here and want to stay, please don't hesitate*

■ *Si* - so

The structure **si** - adjective - **que** requires the subjunctive:

est-il si bavard que tu n'aies pu parler?	*is he so talkative that you were unable to speak?*

Si bien que can have several meanings:

si bien que nous sommes partis	*and so we left*
si bien qu'ils soient, je ne les achète pas	*however good they are, I won't buy them*
il l'a fait si bien qu'il a gagné	*he did it so well that he won*

■ The Subjunctive

The French subjunctive is much more used than its English counterpart. The principal concept of the Subjunctive is that it is used to indicate some element of doubt. It can also indicate emotion or intention. In cases where use of the Subjunctive is optional, an emphasis on uncertainty or intention is best rendered by the Subjunctive and an emphasis on factualness by the Indicative or Conditional. The Subjunctive can also be avoided sometimes by using a straightforward infinitive construction (e.g. **je tiens à le faire, je suis content d'être arrivé**) or a preposition and a noun (e.g. **avant mon arrivée**).

Use the Subjunctive in the following instances:

A. In relative clauses following **que**, when the main clause expresses:

1. Intention, desire, obligation, e.g. after

> **vouloir que**
> **préférer que**
> **désirer que**
> **dire que** (only when intention is implied)
> **avoir soin que**
> **avoir besoin que**
> **insister pour que**
> **exiger que**
> **attendre que**
> **demander que**
> **permettre que**
> **tenir à ce que**
> **espérer que** (though only when used negatively or interrogatively)

– and after the impersonal constructions:

> **il faut que**
> **il importe que**
> **il suffit que**
> **il vaut mieux que**
> **il convient que**
> **il est (grand) temps que**
> **il est nécessaire que**
> **il est important que**
> **il est essentiel que**
> **il est préférable que**
> **il est utile que**

and after the adverbial

assez grand/vieux/etc pour que

Examples:

j'insiste pour qu'elles viennent demain
elle dit qu'il vienne (= she tells him to come; cf. **elle dit qu'il vient,** she says
he is coming)
il est grand temps qu'elle s'en rende compte

2. Denial, avoidance, e.g. after

nier que (unless negative)
ne pas dire que (unless clearly fact: e.g. **ne pas dis que tu es Pierre**)
éviter que
empêcher que
refuser que

and after the impersonal expressions

ce n'est pas que
ce n'est pas la peine que
il est impossible que
il n'est pas possible que
il n'est pas vrai que
il est invraisemble que
il est impensable que
il s'en faut de beaucoup que

Examples:

je nie qu'il ait ces qualités
ce n'est pas qu'il soit tard, mais je dois travailler demain

3. Emotion, judgment: e.g. after

approuver que
accepter que
regretter que
être content/satisfait/etc que
avoir de la chance que
chance encore que
s'étonner que
craindre que

and after the impersonal constructions

il est bon/naturel/juste/normal/bizarre/etc **que**
c'est dommage que
peu (m') importe que and
peu s'en faut que ... ne.

Note: **craindre** is followed by **ne** in the affirmative and not the negative; **ne** is optional in the interrogative.

Examples:

nous avons de la chance qu'il fasse beau
j'ai peur qu'il lui soit arrivé quelque chose

4. Uncertainty, e.g. after

douter que (unless used negatively)
penser croire que (only when used negatively or interrogatively)
supposer que
comprendre que
admettre que
s'expliquer que

and after the impersonal expressions

il paraît que
il est possible/douteux/peu probable/rare que
il arrive que
il n'est pas sûr/certain/il se peut que

Note: the following do not take the Subjunctive:

il est certain/évident/probable/etc **que.**

Examples:

je doute qu'il soit si riche
je comprends qu'il soit venu (= I hear he has come; cf. **je comprends qu'il est venu**, I understand that he has come)

B. After certain conjunctions expressing:

1. Intention:

afin que
pour que

en sorte que
de (telle) sorte/manière/façon que (but use the Indicative or Conditional if a result is implied, rather than an aim: e.g. **il a agi en sorte qu'elle ne pouvait pas sortir**).

Example:

il a agi en sorte qu'elle ne vienne pas

2. Denial:

non (pas) que
pas que
sans que
pas jusqu'à

Examples:

le pire est non qu'il ait pu devenir président, mais qu'il ait pu le rester, the worst of it is not that he could become president but that he could remain it
pas que je sache, not that I know
il n'y a pas jusqu'aux enfants qui ne le sachent, the children know that

3. Condition, contingency, one thing before another:

quoique
bien que
à moins que ... ne
pourvu que
(pour) autant que
de crainte
de peur que
à condition que (this may also take the Future or Conditional)
supposé que
en supposant que
en admettant que
si tant est que
avant que ... ne
en attendant que
jusqu'à ce que

(*not until* should be translated by **pas avant que ... ne** – see below)

and also in the following constructions:

si (+ Indicative) **... que** (repeating and replacing **si**)

que... (et)
soit que ... soit que ...

Examples:

autant que j'en puisse juger, as far as I can tell
si tant est qu'il vienne, je partirai, if he is really coming, I'll leave
qu'il fasse beau, (et) j'irai me promener, if the weather is good, I'll go for a
  walk
qu'il vienne ou pas, ce n'est pas grave, whether he comes or not, it doesn't
  matter
attendez que je vienne, wait until I come (avoid **pas jusqu'à ce que**)
ne parlez pas avant qu'il n'ait fini, don't speak until he has finished

Note that the following do not take the Subjunctive:

au cas où, dans le cas où, au moment où, étant donné que, après que

C. In miscellaneous constructions:

1. Intention, usually but not always with an indefinite article, e.g.

trouvez-moi un notaire qui puisse m'aider
je désire un livre qui me fasse voyager
  cf. **j'ai trouvé un notaire qui peut m'aider** (i.e. result not intention)
trouvez-moi le notaire que je connais (intention, but not any member of the
  class)
j'ai un livre qui me fait voyager (i.e. result)

2. In superlative or restrictive expressions:

After superlative adjectives (e.g. **le plus jeune**) and adjectives with a superlative
quality (e.g. **le premier, dernier, seul, unique,** though not with **fois**):

c'est le meilleur homme que je connaisse

but

c'est le meilleur des hommes que je connais
c'est la première fois que je fais du judo

In restrictive expressions:

il n'y a personnne qui le sache
il y a peu de gens qui le sachent

3. After indefinite relatives (-*ever* contructions):

Examples:

quelques idées que vous ayez
quelles que soient vos idées
quelque courageux qu'ils soient
qui que vous soyez
quoi que vous fassiez
où que vous alliez

but

partout où vous cherchez

4. In set phrases,inversion, ellipsis etc

coûte que coûte, at all costs
grand bien te fasse! much good may it do you!
à Dieu ne plaise! Heaven forbid!
sachez que ... you must realise that
que tu veuilles ou non, whether you like it or not
qu'elle soit triste, c'est sûr, that she is sad is certain
qu'elle le fasse tout de suite, she must do it immediately
puissiez-vous venir! if only you could come!

Tenses required:

In spoken French, use the Present Subjunctive for the present, Future and even the Past. For the Past, the Perfect Subjunctive is also used.

In written French, the same applies, except that it is possible to use the Imperfect Subjunctive if it happens to be in the third person singular. The Pluperfect Subjunctive should be avoided.

Note the following examples of Subjunctive usage:

que tu veuilles ou non	whether you like it or not
pour autant que je sache	as far as I know
je ne sache pas que je vous ai invité	I didn't know that I invited you
sachez que...	you must realise that...
il est important qu'il ait plus d'une personne qui lui soit fidèle	it is important that he has more than one person who is loyal to him (i.e. two separate cases for using the Subjunctive in the same sentence)

refusant que son identité soit dévoilée...	refusing to let his identity be revealed...
cela ne signifiait nullement que la question fût simple	that didn't at all mean that the question was simple
ce n'est pas qu'il soit indifférent à l'argent	it is not that he's indifferent to money
on s'explique assez mal que la situation ait été négligée	it is quite hard to explain how the situation has been neglected
l'art est ce qu'on veut qu'il soit	art is what you want it to be

■ Tenses

These examples show unexpected use of verb tenses:

1. Conditional

si j'étais riche je voyagerais	if I were rich I would travel
moi je vous aurais menti!	would I lie to you?
tu serais un indien, je serais un cowboy	you be an indian, I'll be a cowboy
elle viendrait que je serais content	if she came, I would be happy (literary)
vous auriez travaillé ici depuis longtemps que cela ne m'étonner ait pas	I wouldn't be surprised if you had been working here for a long time
quand (bien) même il s'habillerait comme un roi, il n'aurait jamais d'élégance	even if he dresses like a king he will never be elegant
le président serait mort au dire d'un porte-parole	according to a spokesman the president is dead
il a l'air d'un homme qui aurait beaucoup souffert	he looks like a man who has suffered a lot
auriez-vous l'adresse, s'il vous plaît?	do you have the address, please?
j'eusse été très déçu	I would have been very disappointed (literary variant of j'aurais été très deçu)

2. Past historic and imperfect

The past historic is used to describe a single action or a specified period in the past. The imperfect describes an unspecified state or repeated action.

Note the following illustrative examples:

leurs réussites pendant cette époque furent nombreuses	their successes during this period were numerous

son règne fut tumultueux	his reign was tumultuous
ceci rendait ses yeux plus frappants	this made her eyes more striking
des châteaux de sable étaient détruits	sandcastles were being knocked down
des châteaux de sable furent détruits	sandcastles were knocked down

3. Perfect

With verbs conjugated with **avoir** the past participle agrees with the preceding direct object, if there is one:

c'est la musique que j'ai entendue	that's the music I heard

Some reflexive verbs have direct pronouns and so require the agreement of the past participle, whereas indirect pronouns do not:

elle s'est excusée	she apologised
elle s'est demandé	she wondered
elles se sont lavées	they washed
elles se sont lavé les mains	they washed their hands
elle s'est blessée au doigt	she hurt her hand

Note the standard agreement in passive constructions:

deux hommes ont été tués	two men have been killed

In phrases such as **vu jouer** (past participle + infinitive verb) there is only an agreement with the preceding direct object if you can replace the infinitive verb with its present participle or the expression **en train de jouer**, e.g.

c'est l'actrice que j'ai vue jouer

which could also be expressed as

c'est l'actrice que j'ai vue en train de jouer

but

c'est la pièce de théâtre que j'ai vu jouer

cannot be replaced by

c'est la pièce de théâtre que j'ai vu en train de jouer

so there is no agreement of **vu** with the feminine **pièce de théâtre**.

■ Tense sequence

The future cannot be used after a past tense; the conditional must be used instead. *He said he will/would come* should be translated with the second verb in the conditional, not the future:

Il disait qu'il viendrait

Quand, lorsque and **dès que** are always followed by a future tense when the main clause is in the future, whereas in English such a subordinate clause may be followed by a future or a present tense.

je sifflerai dès qu'elle commencera à *I shall whistle as soon as she starts*
chanter   *singing*

Note the following construction after **quand, lorsque, à peine, après que, aussitôt que, dès que** with the use of the past anterior, followed by the past historic:

après qu'il eut roté, il devint tout *after he had burped he went all red*
rouge

In spoken French this would be rendered as:

après qu'il a eu roté, il est devenu tout rouge

If it is a habitual action, the pluperfect should be used:

après qu'il avait roté, il devenait *after he burped he went all red*
tout rouge

■ Verbs 1 - verb formation

The following are areas of potential error in verbal usage. They are divided into three groups: **-er**, **-ir** and **-re** verbs.

1. **-er** verbs

 – third person plural present of **fonder**: **ils fondent**
 – third person plural past historic **fonder**: **ils fondèrent**

2. **-ir** verbs

 – first person singular future of **mourir**: **je mourrai** (not **mourirai**)
 – third person plural imperfect of **courir**: **ils couraient** (not **courraient**)
 – third person plural future of **courir**: **ils courront**
 – first person singular present/past historic of **voir**: **je vois/vis**

3. **-re** verbs

 – third person singular past historic of **descendre, répondre**: **il descendit, répondit** (not **descenda, réponda**)
 – first person singular present of **mettre**: **je mets** (not **mis**)
 – first person singular past historic of **écrire**: **j'écrivis** (not **écris**)

- third person plural present of **fondre: ils fondent**
- third person plural past historic **fondre: ils fondirent**
- past participle of **rire, mettre, écrire: ri, mis, écrit** (same sound but three different spellings)
- first person singular present/past historic of **vivre: je vis/vécus**

Verbs take a circumflex in the first and second person plural of the past historic and the third person singular of the pluperfect subjunctive only. See p 121 for modal verb conjugations.

■ Verbs 2 - changes of spelling

1. Verbs ending -**cer**:

   c becomes **ç** before **a**, **o** or **u**, e.g.

   il commença

2. Verbs ending in -**ger**:

   g becomes **ge** before **a**, **o** or **u**, e.g.

   nous mangeons

3. Verbs ending -**eler** and -**eter**:

   l becomes **ll** and **t** becomes **tt** before a mute **e**, e.g.

   épeler - j'épelle
   jeter - je jette

4. Verbs ending in -**ayer/-oyer/-uyer**:

   y becomes **i** before a mute **e**, e.g.

   délayer - je délaie
   nettoyer - je nettoie
   essuyer - j'essuie

5. Verbs ending in **e**-consonant-**er**:

   e becomes **è** before a mute **e**, e.g.

   acheter - j'achète

6. Verbs ending in **é**-consonant-**er**:

   é becomes **e** before a mute **e**, e.g.

   espérer - j'espère

■ Verbs 3 - imperatives

-er verbs do not take an s inthe second person singular imperative, except in cases of elision, i.e.

donne!   parle!   va!

but   **donnes-en!**   give some!
           parles-en!   talk about it!
           vas-y   go on!

AVOIR
to have

PRESENT	**IMPERFECT**	**FUTURE**
j'ai	j'avais	j'aurai
tu as	tu avais	tu auras
il a	il avait	il aura
nous avons	nous avions	nous aurons
vous avez	vous aviez	vous aurez
ils ont	ils avaient	ils auront

PAST HISTORIC	**PERFECT**	**PLUPERFECT**
j'eus	j'ai eu	j'avais eu
tu eus	tu as eu	tu avais eu
il eut	il a eu	il avait eu
nous eûmes	nous avons eu	nous avions eu
vous eûtes	vous avez eu	vous aviez eu
ils eurent	ils ont eu	ils avaient eu

CONDITIONAL

PAST ANTERIOR	**PRESENT**	**PAST**
j'eus eu etc	j'aurais	j'aurais eu
	tu aurais	tu aurais eu
	il aurait	il aurait eu
	nous aurions	nous aurions eu
FUTURE PERFECT	vous auriez	vous auriez eu
j'aurai eu etc	ils auraient	ils auraient eu

SUBJUNCTIVE

PRESENT	**IMPERFECT**	**PLUPERFECT**
j'aie	j'eusse	j'aie eu
tu aies	tu eusses	tu aies eu
il ait	il eût	il ait eu
nous ayons	nous eussions	nous ayons eu
vous ayez	vous eussiez	vous ayez eu
ils aient	ils eussent	ils aient eu

IMPERATIVE	*INFINITIVE*	*PARTICIPLE*
aie	**PRESENT**	**PRESENT**
ayons	avoir	ayant
ayez		
	PAST	**PAST**
	avoir eu	eu

DEVOIR
to have to

PRESENT	IMPERFECT	FUTURE
je dois	je devais	je devrai
tu dois	tu devais	tu devras
il doit	il devait	il devra
nous devons	nous devions	nous devrons
vous devez	vous deviez	vous devrez
ils doivent	ils devaient	ils devront

PAST HISTORIC	PERFECT	PLUPERFECT
je dus	j'ai dû	j'avais dû
tu dus	tu as dû	tu avais dû
il dut	il a dû	il avait dû
nous dûmes	nous avons dû	nous avions dû
vous dûtes	vous avez dû	vous aviez dû
ils durent	ils ont dû	ils avaient dû

	CONDITIONAL	
PAST ANTERIOR	**PRESENT**	**PAST**
j'eus dû etc	je devrais	j'aurais dû
	tu devrais	tu aurais dû
	il devrait	il aurait dû
	nous devrions	nous aurions dû
FUTURE PERFECT	vous devriez	vous auriez dû
j'aurai dû etc	ils devraient	ils auraient dû

SUBJUNCTIVE

PRESENT	IMPERFECT	PLUPERFECT
je doive	je dusse	j'aie dû
tu doives	tu dusses	tu aies dû
il doive	il dût	il ait dû
nous devions	nous dussions	nous ayons dû
vous deviez	vous dussiez	vous ayez dû
ils doivent	ils dussent	ils aient dû

IMPERATIVE	*INFINITIVE*	*PARTICIPLE*
dois	**PRESENT**	**PRESENT**
devons	devoir	devant
devez		
	PAST	**PAST**
	avoir dû	dû

ETRE
to be

PRESENT	IMPERFECT	FUTURE
je suis	j'étais	je serai
tu es	tu étais	tu seras
il est	il était	il sera
nous sommes	nous étions	nous serons
vous êtes	vous étiez	vous serez
ils sont	ils étaient	ils seront

PAST HISTORIC	PERFECT	PLUPERFECT
je fus	j'ai été	j'avais été
tu fus	tu as été	tu avais été
il fut	il a été	il avait été
nous fûmes	nous avons été	nous avions été
vous fûtes	vous avez été	vous aviez été
ils furent	ils ont été	ils avaient été

CONDITIONAL

PAST ANTERIOR	PRESENT	PAST
j'eus été etc	je serais	j'aurais été
	tu serais	tu aurais été
	il serait	il aurait été
	nous serions	nous aurions été
FUTURE PERFECT	vous seriez	vous auriez été
j'aurai été etc	ils seraient	ils auraient été

SUBJUNCTIVE

PRESENT	IMPERFECT	PLUPERFECT
je sois	je fusse	j'aie été
tu sois	tu fusses	tu aies été
il soit	il fût	il ait été
nous soyons	nous fussions	nous ayons été
vous soyez	vous fussiez	vous ayez été
ils soient	ils fussent	ils aient été

IMPERATIVE / INFINITIVE / PARTICIPLE

IMPERATIVE	INFINITIVE	PARTICIPLE
sois	**PRESENT**	**PRESENT**
soyons	être	étant
soyez		
	PAST	**PAST**
	avoir été	été

FAIRE
to do, to make

PRESENT	IMPERFECT	FUTURE
je fais	je faisais	je ferai
tu fais	tu faisais	tu feras
il fait	il faisait	il fera
nous faisons	nous faisions	nous ferons
vous faites	vous faisiez	vous ferez
ils font	ils faisaient	ils feront

PAST HISTORIC	PERFECT	PLUPERFECT
je fis	j'ai fait	j'avais fait
tu fis	tu as fait	tu avais fait
il fit	il a fait	il avait fait
nous fîmes	nous avons fait	nous avions fait
vous fîtes	vous avez fait	vous aviez fait
ils firent	ils ont fait	ils avaient fait

CONDITIONAL

PAST ANTERIOR	PRESENT	PAST
j'eus fait etc	je ferais	j'aurais fait
	tu ferais	tu aurais fait
	il ferait	il aurait fait
	nous ferions	nous aurions fait
FUTURE PERFECT	vous feriez	vous auriez fait
j'aurai fait etc	ils feraient	ils auraient fait

SUBJUNCTIVE

PRESENT	IMPERFECT	PLUPERFECT
je fasse	je fisse	j'aie fait
tu fasses	tu fisses	tu aies fait
il fasse	il fît	il ait fait
nous fassions	nous fissions	nous ayons fait
vous fassiez	vous fissiez	vous ayez fait
ils fassent	ils fissent	ils aient fait

IMPERATIVE

fais
faisons
faites

INFINITIVE

PRESENT
faire

PAST
avoir fait

PARTICIPLE

PRESENT
faisant

PAST
fait

FALLOIR
to be necessary

PRESENT	IMPERFECT	FUTURE
il faut	il fallait	il faudra

PAST HISTORIC	PERFECT	PLUPERFECT
il fallut	il a fallu	il avait fallu

	CONDITIONAL	
PAST ANTERIOR	**PRESENT**	**PAST**
il eut fallu		
	il faudrait	il aurait fallu
FUTURE PERFECT		
il aura fallu		

SUBJUNCTIVE

PRESENT	IMPERFECT	PLUPERFECT
il faille	il fallût	il ait fallu

IMPERATIVE	*INFINITIVE*	*PARTICIPLE*
	PRESENT falloir	**PRESENT**
	PAST avoir fallu	**PAST** fallu

POUVOIR
to be able to

PRESENT	IMPERFECT	FUTURE
je peux	je pouvais	je pourrai
tu peux	tu pouvais	tu pourras
il peut	il pouvait	il pourra
nous pouvons	nous pouvions	nous pourrons
vous pouvez	vous pouviez	vous pourrez
ils peuvent	ils pouvaient	ils pourront

PAST HISTORIC	PERFECT	PLUPERFECT
je pus	j'ai pu	j'avais pu
tu pus	tu as pu	tu avais pu
il put	il a pu	il avait pu
nous pûmes	nous avons pu	nous avions pu
vous pûtes	vous avez pu	vous aviez pu
ils purent	ils ont pu	ils avaient pu

CONDITIONAL

PAST ANTERIOR	PRESENT	PAST
j'eus pu etc	je pourrais	j'aurais pu
	tu pourrais	tu aurais pu
	il pourrait	il aurait pu
	nous pourrions	nous aurions pu
FUTURE PERFECT	vous pourriez	vous auriez pu
j'aurai pu etc	ils pourraient	ils auraient pu

SUBJUNCTIVE

PRESENT	IMPERFECT	PLUPERFECT
je puisse	je pusse	j'aie pu
tu puisses	tu pusses	tu aies pu
il puisse	il pût	il ait pu
nous puissions	nous pussions	nous ayonspu
vous puissiez	vous pussiez	vous ayez pu
ils puissent	ils pussent	ils aient pu

IMPERATIVE	INFINITIVE	PARTICIPLE
	PRESENT	PRESENT
	pouvoir	pouvant
pouvez		
	PAST	PAST
	avoir pu	pu

VOULOIR
to want

PRESENT	IMPERFECT	FUTURE
je veux	je voulais	je voudrai
tu veux	tu voulais	tu voudras
il veut	il voulait	il voudra
nous voulons	nous voulions	nous voudrons
vous voulez	vous vouliez	vous voudrez
ils veulent	ils voulaient	ils voudront

PAST HISTORIC	PERFECT	PLUPERFECT
je voulus	j'ai voulu	j'avais voulu
tu voulus	tu as voulu	tu avais voulu
il voulut	il a voulu	il avait voulu
nous voulûmes	nous avons voulu	nous avions voulu
vous voulûtes	vous avez voulu	vous aviez voulu
ils voulurent	ils ont voulu	ils avaient voulu

CONDITIONAL

PAST ANTERIOR	PRESENT	PAST
j'eus voulu etc	je voudrais	j'aurais voulu
	tu voudrais	tu aurais voulu
	il voudrait	il aurait voulu
	nous voudrions	nous aurions voulu
FUTURE PERFECT	vous voudriez	vous auriez voulu
j'aurai voulu etc	ils voudraient	ils auraient voulu

SUBJUNCTIVE

PRESENT	IMPERFECT	PLUPERFECT
je veuille	je voulusse	j'aie voulu
tu veuilles	tu voulusses	tu aies voulu
il veuille	il voulût	il ait voulu
nous voulions	nous voulussions	nous ayons voulu
vous vouliez	vous voulussiez	vous ayez voulu
ils veuillent	ils voulussent	ils aient voulu

IMPERATIVE	INFINITIVE	PARTICIPLE
veuille	**PRESENT**	**PRESENT**
veuillons	vouloir	voulant
veuilez		
	PAST	**PAST**
	avoir voulu	voulu